Finding
Significance

W9-CHQ-858

Finding Significance

Adessa Holden

MORNING JOY MEDIA
Spring City, Pennsylvania

Copyright © 2015 Adessa Holden

All rights reserved. No portion of this book may be reproduced, stored in a retrieval system, or transmitted in any form or by any means—electronic, mechanical, photocopy, recording, scanning, or other—except for brief quotations in reviews or articles, without the prior written permission of the author.

Published by Morning Joy Media.

Visit www.morningjoymedia.com for more information on bulk discounts and special promotions, or e-mail your questions to info@morningjoymedia.com.

All Scripture quotations, unless otherwise indicated, are taken from the Holy Bible, New International Version®, NIV®. Copyright ©1973, 1978, 1984, 2011 by Biblica, Inc.™ Used by permission of Zondervan. All rights reserved worldwide. www.zondervan.com The "NIV" and "New International Version" are trademarks registered in the United States Patent and Trademark Office by Biblica, Inc.™

Scripture verses marked KJV are from the King James Version of the Bible.

The Prayer of Confession and Deliverance originates with Rev. Richard Herritt of Herritt Spiritual Warfare Ministries, Inc., www.conquerors-in-christ.org. Used by permission.

Design: Debbie Capeci

Subject Headings:

1. Self-esteem—Religious aspects—Christianity. 2. Christian life. 3. Christian women—Religious life. I. Title.

ISBN 978-1-937107-41-3 (paperback)
ISBN 978-1-937107-42-0 (ebook)

Printed in the United States of America

*I'd like to dedicate this book to my mom, Kathy Holden,
who taught my brother and I through her words and her life
that there is nothing more important than
developing a personal relationship with Jesus
and finding our significance in Him.*

Contents

Chapter 1

Finding Significance in a Stable

Ordinary.

Insignificant.

Unsophisticated.

Working-class.

Unimportant.

Crude.

*T*hese are just some of the words the priests and religious leaders used to refer to the people that lived in Nazareth. Actually, these were the nice words they used. They also used more derogatory words, but they all meant basically the same thing: The inhabitants of Nazareth did not measure up to those who lived in Judea.

The Nazarenes were the small-town country cousins. They were an embarrassment. They didn't have the training, the learning, or the religious piety of the inhabitants of Judea. They were "the people up north." As one celebrated Rabbi was known to pray, "I thank Thee, O Lord my God and God of my fathers, that Thou has cast my lot among those who frequent the schools and synagogues, and not among those who attend the theatre and circus. For, both I and they work and watch—I to inherit eternal life, they for their destruction."[1]

Perhaps Nathaniel sums it up best when he says, **"Nazareth! Can anything good come from there?" (John 1:46).** For sure, Nazareth wasn't Jerusalem. It couldn't claim the heritage of being the city of the great King David. It didn't house the temple. It wasn't the center of Jewish worship. Absolutely no one in the religious community was looking for a move of God to start in Nazareth.

It wasn't just the Jewish religious leaders who viewed this tiny town as a nuisance. The only time Nazareth drew any attention from the Roman government was when there was an uprising. There certainly were enough of them!

You see, even though its citizens didn't live up to the standards of the religious Jewish hierarchy, they were still extremely nationalistic. They hated the Roman government. This town wasn't known for producing diplomats or world leaders. No, Nazareth was known to produce terrorists—zealous Jews who wanted to overthrow the Roman government at any price.

Still, the Roman government didn't really take them seriously. How was this tiny town going to overthrow an entire empire? Rather than stressing about it, Rome dropped the hammer on it and filled it with Roman soldiers who beat all the young men—especially the Jews. To the Roman government, Nazareth was an annoyance, but not a threat. They certainly didn't expect a great ruler to come from it. Really, they didn't expect anything but trouble. That's all anyone expected from Nazareth. Everyone except God.

When God looked at the small town of Nazareth, he saw potential. When he was orchestrating the events and choosing the people who would participate in the greatest miracle in the history of the world, he didn't choose anyone who lived in Jerusalem or Rome. He didn't choose the virgin daughter of the high priest or a young man who was Jewish-born but Roman-educated. No, he chose a young couple from the no-good, unsophisticated, country town of Nazareth.

> **In the sixth month of Elizabeth's pregnancy, God sent the angel Gabriel to Nazareth, a town in Galilee, to a virgin pledged to be married to a man named Joseph, a descendant of David.**
>
> **The virgin's name was Mary.**
>
> **The angel went to her and said, "Greetings, you who are highly favored! The Lord is with you" (Luke 1:26–28).**

"Highly-favored."

Before this very moment, Mary never would have used these words to describe herself. She would have used words like, "normal, ordinary, young, and yes, Nazarene." All the descriptions that went with the town of Nazareth belonged to her, because this was her hometown.

The truth was that she was just a small-town girl raised to be a wife and mother and spend the rest of her life raising her family in the small town of Nazareth. She was just like every other girl living in Nazareth—no special skills or training. No one would have picked her out of a crowd and said, "She's going to play a part in God's plan to revolu-

God saw something in Mary's heart he could use.

tionize the world." No one saw anything significant in Mary. No one except God.

God saw something in Mary's heart that he could use. On an ordinary day, while Mary was performing her mundane chores, the angel Gabriel visited her with the message:

"Greetings, you who are highly favored! The Lord is with you... Do not be afraid, Mary; you have found favor with God. You will conceive and give birth to a son, and you are to call him Jesus. He will be great and will be called the Son of the Most High. The Lord God will give him the throne of his father David, and he will reign over Jacob's descendants forever; his kingdom will never end" (Luke 1:28–33).

Can you imagine what must have been racing through Mary's mind?

I know if I were in her shoes, I'd have only caught some phrases as I stood there in complete shock and awe. Let's look at some of the phrases her mind had to choose from:

"You are highly favored of God."

Me? An insignificant, young girl from Nazareth?

"You have found favor with God."

How? All I've done is live a normal life and try to do my best to please him.

"You will conceive and have a son."

Okay, we know that one shocked her because she asks the angel how that is going to happen.

"He will be great. He will be called the Son of the Most High God. He will reign on the throne of David and over Jacob's descendants. His kingdom will never end."

Mind-blowing.

Do you think she could even take it all in as she listened to what she was being told? I mean, imagine it: she's your average, young, small-town girl. A virgin, being told not only that she's going to miraculously conceive a baby, but that this baby is God's own Son, the promised Messiah! Even though every nativity reenactment I've ever seen presents Mary as calm and almost angel-like, I wonder if at some point in this conversation she didn't have to sit down before she said:

"How will this be," Mary asked the angel, "since I am a virgin?"

The angel answered, "The Holy Spirit will come on you, and the power of the Most High will overshadow you. So the holy one to be born will be called the Son of God. Even Elizabeth your relative is going to have a child in her old age, and she who was said to be unable to conceive is in her sixth month. For no word from God will ever fail" (Luke 1:34–37).

Can you imagine? Here she is a young, inexperienced, Nazarene girl being told that her entire life is about to change. Certainly throughout her life she'd heard about God's promises to send a Messiah to save his people. She may have even known that it was prophesied the Messiah would be born of a virgin. But could she have ever thought SHE would be the chosen girl?

Still, in that moment it didn't matter. The hows, the whys, the what-ifs didn't matter. What mattered is that God had chosen her. He wanted her. If he wanted her, than she was his.

"I am the Lord's servant," Mary answered. "May your word to me be fulfilled." Then the angel left her (Luke 1:38).

That day in the backward town despised by both the Jewish and the Roman officials, God took an insignificant young woman and he gave her a significant place in his kingdom.

Of course, Mary wasn't the only one involved in this story. We must remember there was a young man from this same small town whose life was turned upside down when Gabriel visited Mary.

This is how the birth of Jesus the Messiah came about: His mother Mary was pledged to be married to Joseph, but before they came together, she was found to be pregnant through the Holy Spirit. Because Joseph her husband was faithful to the law, and yet did not want to expose her to public disgrace, he had in mind to divorce her quietly (Matthew 1:18–19).

Then there was Joseph. Here was a righteous young man who thought he had his life pretty well planned out. His trade was set—he'd be a carpenter. He was planning on marrying Mary and raising a family. He expected a normal, happy life.

Then he heard Mary was pregnant. Suddenly, his life was in shambles. How could this happen? Who was the father of Mary's child? What was he going to do? He wrestled with the questions of right and wrong, and how to handle the matter until he came to a decision. However, before he could act on the decision, he received an angelic visitation explaining the miracle that was happening.

But after he had considered this, an angel of the Lord appeared to him in a dream and said, "Joseph son of David, do not be afraid to take Mary home as your wife, because what is conceived in her is from the Holy Spirit. She will give birth to

a son, and you are to give him the name Jesus, because he will save his people from their sins."

All this took place to fulfill what the Lord had said through the prophet: "The virgin will conceive and give birth to a son, and they will call him Immanuel" (which means "God with us") (Matthew 1:20–23).

With the angel's visit, everything changed. Suddenly, Joseph's life went from normal, obscure, and predictable to absolutely unbelievable. But the amazing thing about Joseph is he believed the angel. He didn't just believe with his head, but he believed enough to obey God and do exactly what the angel told him to do.

When Joseph woke up, he did what the angel of the Lord had commanded him and took Mary home as his wife. But he did not consummate their marriage until she gave birth to a son. And he gave him the name Jesus (Matthew 1:24–25).

Just like Mary, Joseph may have been living an ordinary life in an ordinary town, but he had an extraordinary heart toward God. He may not have had much formal education— he wasn't trained in religion like a priest or Pharisee or in the ways of Rome or Greek philosophy. His training came in the form of an apprenticeship in carpentry. Still, God chose him to be Jesus' father and to teach Jesus God's ways.

Did you ever wonder why? I believe it's because God wasn't looking for someone with a lot of head knowledge, He wanted his Son to be raised by a man who had an intimate, personal relationship with him.

That was Joseph. He knew what God wanted and he did it—end of story. God wanted Jesus raised by a man who could hear his voice and who would follow him wherever he led. He wasn't concerned about Joseph's formal education. He saw his heart was the heart of a man he could use. That was the character trait that qualified an insignificant carpenter to play a significant role in raising the Son of God.

You see, when God is choosing people to work in his kingdom, he isn't going through resumes or looking for all the right qualifications. He isn't looking for a certain age, gender, or ethnicity. He's looking for people who will love him with all of their hearts, souls, and minds, and commit all of their strength to following him. He's looking for empty vessels that will say, "I may not have much to give, Lord, but whatever I have, you can use for your honor and glory."

God is looking for empty vessels who will say "I don't have a lot to give, but whatever I have, you can use for your glory!"

He's searching for people who will allow him to change them into the image of his Son without reservation. He's seeking people who will follow him whenever, wherever, and do whatever he commands. He's looking for obedience, humility, and a heart that is fully committed to him. As we see over and over again in the story of Jesus' birth, God loves to speak significance into the lives of people who are hungry for him, even though the rest of the world has written them off as insignificant.

Perhaps no one demonstrates this truth as well as the shepherds who visited the stable the night Jesus was born. In New Testament times, shepherding was not considered a good livelihood. In fact, Jewish wisdom during the time of

Jesus' birth advised fathers against shepherding as an occupation for their sons. Shepherds were looked down upon, not trusted, even scorned. They were often peripheral to Jewish life and culture.

They were outcasts. Lowlifes. They were from the class of people you don't invite to parties. They weren't part of the "in crowd" of synagogues or social groups. Honestly, most people didn't want anything to do with shepherds at all.

Still, the shepherds were the only ones God invited to the birth of Jesus the Savior and Lord! They were the only group of people honored to hear the heavenly chorus of angels announcing, "Glory to God in the Highest." Among all the crowds in Bethlehem, they were the only people that abandoned their prior commitments and went to the stable to worship Jesus. By extending this private invitation to the shepherds, God was saying, "Everyone is welcome in my kingdom. No one is too socially unacceptable to be used in my plan."

The prophetess Anna is another example of God honoring and involving people that may be seen as unimportant, peripheral, and insignificant in the eyes of the world, but who to him have outstanding character traits. Anna was just a young woman when tragedy changed her life. She had only been married for seven years when her husband died. Knowing the standard marrying age at this time, you can assume Anna was no more than twenty-one years old when he died.

Widowhood in that society was very difficult. It virtually guaranteed a life of extreme poverty. Still, Anna didn't use this tragedy as an occasion to be angry with God. Instead, she devoted the rest of her life to serving God. She literally moved into the temple and devoted the next sixty-four years of her life to prayer, fasting, and teaching other women the Bible.

Don't think her years of sacrifice and devotion to God went unnoticed! One day while Anna was praying in the temple, the Holy Spirit led her to the exact place where Mary and Joseph were dedicating Jesus.

> **There was also a prophet, Anna, the daughter of Penuel, of the tribe of Asher. She was very old; she had lived with her husband seven years after her marriage, and then was a widow until she was eighty-four. She never left the temple but worshiped night and day, fasting and praying. Coming up to them at that very moment, she gave thanks to God and spoke about the child to all who were looking forward to the redemption of Jerusalem (Luke 2:36–38).**

What an honor this was for Anna! To see the long-awaited Messiah with her own eyes! No doubt over the years she'd prayed that the Messiah would come and deliver his people, Israel. Now she was seeing the answer to her prayers. Among all the great priests, religious leaders, and kings in Jerusalem who would have been more than happy to tell you how important they were, God chose Anna to play a significant role at his Son's dedication. What a privilege God gave Anna in allowing her to see the Messiah and tell her story to other people who were also waiting for the promised Messiah.

The ironic thing is the big, successful, important religious leaders missed the whole thing. There were no religious rulers from the important town of Jerusalem gathered around the manger. Although they may have walked by, there were no Pharisees or Sadducees participating in Christ's dedication. No Roman government officials saw the angels singing at night or stopped collecting taxes long enough to notice that the very essence of the cosmos had just changed.

Think about it: The Son of God came to earth in the form of a man with the express purpose of offering redemption and eternal life to all who would believe in him. It was a miraculous, revolutionary, cataclysmic event. Still, the only people involved were a poor young couple from a small, insignificant town, a few insignificant shepherds, and two elderly people at the temple.

Would anyone besides God have planned it this way?

Never.

However, this is one of God's trademarks.

He sees significance where the world sees insignificance.

He sees potential where others see nothing.

Where others see no hope, he speaks new life.

He sees beyond the standards that the world uses to judge people, and he focuses on the heart. He looks beyond the labels others have placed on you and he calls you, "My precious daughter."

No matter what labels others have given you, your heavenly Father says, **"But you are a chosen people, a royal priesthood, a holy nation, God's special possession, that you may declare the praises of him who called you out of darkness into his wonderful light" (1 Peter 2:9).**

Perhaps people have spoken words about you that sound a lot like what Nathaniel said about Nazareth, "Can anything good come from her?"

Thankfully, the answer is the same today as it was two thousand years ago.

Absolutely YES!

Because the same God that looked beyond the rough exterior of that small town and saw the hearts of two young people willing to do whatever he asked sees past whatever boundaries are standing in your path and sees your heart.

Just like he had a purpose for their lives, he has a plan and a purpose for you.

The same God who called the shepherds to the stable is calling you today. He is saying, **"Come and see the plans I have for you. The plans I have laid from the foundations of the world. See yourself through my eyes, and join me on the adventure I have for you."**

Like he did for Mary, Joseph, the shepherds, and Anna, the God of the universe is inviting you to find your place of significance in the center of his plan for your life.

The choice is yours. Will you answer his invitation?

Chapter 1 Questions

1. **With which person in this chapter can you identify most?**

2. **What about his or her story stood out to you?**

3. **Have you ever felt insignificant or unprepared for a challenge or opportunity God placed in your life?**

4. **What role did obedience play in each person's life?**

5. **How do you think their choices to live for God in their normal, average lives prepared them for the time when God called them to become part of his extraordinary miracle?**

6. **What did this chapter teach you about finding your own significant plan in God's kingdom?**

Chapter 2

He Was a Man
of No Reputation

*M*ost of us have either experienced this scene or seen it on television:

"UGGHHH!!!!"

"Just keep pushing—you're almost there."

"I can see the head, keep pushing, you're almost done."

After one more push, combined with a cry of pain from the mother, the sound of a baby's cry fills the air as a new baby boy breathes in his first whiff of air.

Have you ever thought about the first thing the baby Jesus smelled as he was welcomed to this planet? As a country girl who lives not too far away from a farm, I don't have to guess. I know exactly what he smelled, and let me tell you—it wasn't pretty!

The first smells that filled his senses weren't fragrant perfumes or gentle aromas. It wasn't even hospital antiseptic. He smelled musty hay, dirty, sweaty animals, and the overwhelming essence of manure! His first visitors weren't exactly wearing sterile hospital gowns either. There's a pretty good chance that the shepherds who came directly from the fields were carrying a distinct odor of their own!

His was a humble beginning. The Son of God born in a stable, not exactly the place you'd expect to find a king. That's what makes the stable, complete with all of its sights and sounds and smells, completely compatible with the life-style Jesus would lead. For although he was the King of Kings and Lord of Lords, when he came to earth he laid all of his rights aside. As Paul says in Philippians 2:6–8,

Who, being in very nature God, did not consider equality with God something to be used to his own advantage; rather, he made himself nothing by taking the very nature of a servant, being made in human likeness. And being found in appearance as a man, he humbled himself by becoming obedient to death—even death on a cross!

From the moment Jesus arrived on the planet, he lived what appeared to be a humble, ordinary, mundane life. True, there were glimpses of greatness from time to time, but for the most part, Jesus lived the first thirty years of his life unnoticed.

He was just another baby, just another child, just another apprentice carpenter, and then just another hard-working man. The King of the universe didn't come to live in a palace. He didn't aspire to lead an uprising that would overthrow the Roman government. He didn't even try to gain influence and popularity among the Jewish religious elite. He was born, he grew, he lived, and he worked among the ordinary, average Joes of his day. It all began when he was born in a stable.

Of course, Mary and Joseph couldn't set up housekeeping in a stable—that's just where Jesus was born. After that one miraculous night, Mary and Joseph began the process of starting a new life in the town of Bethlehem. They found a house. Joseph used his skills as a carpenter to support them. Jesus spent his days just like any other baby—eating, sleeping, and pooping in his diapers. Under Mary's care, he learned about the world around him, laughed, cried, and played. For the most part, they were just your average young family living in Bethlehem.

Then a glimpse of greatness interrupted their lives again.

After Jesus was born in Bethlehem in Judea, during the time of King Herod, Magi from the east came to Jerusalem and asked, "Where is the one who has been born king of the Jews? We saw his star when it rose and have come to worship him."

When King Herod heard this he was disturbed, and all Jerusalem with him. When he had called together all the people's chief priests and teachers of the law, he asked them where the Messiah was to be born.

"In Bethlehem in Judea," they replied, "for this is what the prophet has written.... Then Herod called the Magi secretly and found out from them the exact time the star had appeared. He sent them to Bethlehem and said, "Go and search carefully for the child. As soon as you find him, report to me, so that I too may go and worship him."

After they had heard the king, they went on their way, and the star they had seen when it rose went ahead of them until it stopped over the place where the child was. When they saw the star, they were overjoyed. On coming to the house, they saw the child with his mother Mary, and they bowed down and worshiped him. Then

**they opened their treasures and presented him
with gifts of gold, frankincense and myrrh. And
having been warned in a dream not to go back to
Herod, they returned to their country by another
route (Matthew 2:1-12).**

Once again, Mary and Joseph's lives were turned upside
down when the wise men interrupted their normal life to
visit Jesus. Honestly, I can't imagine what it must have been
like for them, constantly moving back and forth between the
ordinary and mundane and the extraordinary and miraculous.

Can you picture it? Let's say that you are Mary. You get
up in the morning thinking you're going to live just another
ordinary day. You make your husband breakfast. You're busy
trying to get your chores done and take care of your baby
when you hear a knock at the door.

Imagine your surprise when you open the door and meet
the wise men. They explain that for three years they've been
following a star that has led them to your home, and they are
here to worship and present gifts to your child.

If she's like most women, at this point she's thinking,
"What does he look like? Did I wash his face? Does he have
a fresh diaper? Look at this house—I was so not ready for
company—especially not magi from the East!"

Then you realize, "This isn't the time to be thinking about
these things." Suddenly, you realize what is happening. Another extraordinary move of God is interrupting your normal
life.

As the wise men start presenting their gifts—gold, frankincense, and myrrh—you're wondering, "What is happening?
Why is this happening? What will come next?"

What happens next is another new beginning, another
new start. You're moving—this time to Egypt.

When they had gone, an angel of the Lord appeared to Joseph in a dream. "Get up," he said, "take the child and his mother and escape to Egypt. Stay there until I tell you, for Herod is going to search for the child to kill him."

So he got up, took the child and his mother during the night and left for Egypt, where he stayed until the death of Herod (Matthew 2:13–15).

Most scholars agree that the young family did not stay in Egypt very long before King Herod died. That's when Joseph experienced this third and final angelic visit.

After Herod died, an angel of the Lord appeared in a dream to Joseph in Egypt and said, "Get up, take the child and his mother and go to the land of Israel, for those who were trying to take the child's life are dead."

So he got up, took the child and his mother and went to the land of Israel. But when he heard that Archelaus was reigning in Judea in place of his father Herod, he was afraid to go there. Having been warned in a dream, he withdrew to the district of Galilee, and he went and lived in a town called Nazareth. So was fulfilled what was said through the prophets, that he would be called a Nazarene (Matthew 2:19–23).

It had been a wild ride! They started in Nazareth and went to Bethlehem. From Bethlehem they went to Egypt. Now from Egypt they went back to Nazareth. Along the way, they'd experienced angelic visitations, a miraculous night in a stable, and the visit of the magi and their gifts. They were the target of the evil Herod's insane murderous rampage. They escaped and hid out in a foreign country. It had been exciting, petrifying, overwhelming, and exhilarating all at the same time.

However, with the final visitation from the angel, all of that was going to change. The excitement was over. The miraculous was again going to be replaced with the mundane. Joseph and Mary were taking their son, probably now a toddler, back home to Nazareth.

From this point on, with the exception of a brief narrative of Jesus at the temple, the Bible is silent about what happened in the life of this young family and the life of Christ. All we know is that they moved to Nazareth and remained there for the rest of Jesus' life. Joseph earned his living as a carpenter and passed that trade on to Jesus. The family grew as more children were added and Jesus **"grew and became strong; he was filled with wisdom, and the grace of God was on him" (Luke 2:40).**

We know from Luke 2:51–52 that after his time at the Jerusalem temple, **"He went down to Nazareth with them and was obedient to them.... And Jesus grew in wisdom and stature, and in favor with God and man."**

It doesn't give a lot of detail, but it gives enough. After all, just saying that he was from Nazareth tells us a lot.

Remember Nazareth? We talked a little bit about it in the previous chapter, but in this chapter, we're going to take a closer look. Most of the information in this section came from Alfred Edersheim's book *The Life and Times of Jesus the Messiah.*[1]

Nazareth was located in the Jewish province of Galilee. While the land of Israel was divided according to tribes in the Old Testament, in the New Testament it was divided into regions. Three of the most familiar regions were Galilee, Samaria, and Judea.

No two regions could ever have been more different than Judea and Galilee. In fact, they were even at opposite ends of Israel geographically—Galilee was to the north and Judea to the south.

Judea was the region of all things religious. It was a dry, infertile region full of rocks and limestone. Many of its ancient cities were ruins.

Edersheim describes it this way:

In Judea all seemed to invite retrospection and introspection; to favor habits of solitary thought and study, til it kindled toward fanaticism. Mile by mile as you travelled southwards, memories of the past would crowd around...the traveler would meet few foreigners, but everywhere encounter those gaunt representatives of what was regarded as the superlative excellency of his religion.[2]

Judea was the home of both Jerusalem and the temple. It was the center of the Jewish religion, and the people from that region took their religion very, very seriously. In fact, they took everything very, very seriously. They held to the absolute strictest version of the Law. This was the region of the Pharisees and Sadducees, religious politics mixed with religious hypocrisy. Needless to say, the Judeans were a proud and haughty people, as is evidenced by the popular saying, "Go north if you want riches, south if you want wisdom." Edersheim says,

The people of Judea believed they were "purer" Jews than the Galileans. They were proud of the fact that they didn't fraternize with Gentiles like the Galileans did.

There was a general contempt in Rabbinic circles for all that was Galilean. They even hated the way the

*people of Galilee spoke. Although the Judean or Je-
rusalem dialect was far from pure, the people of Galilee were especially blamed for neglecting the study of
their language, charged with errors in grammar, and
especially with absurd mispronunciation, sometimes
leading to ridiculous mistakes.[3]*

"Galilean—Fool" was one of their favorite expressions.

Truly, Judea was the land of the snob, the self-absorbed,
and the self-proclaimed religiously sophisticated. Galilee, on
the other hand, was a completely different story. Whereas
Judea was a barren land full of ancient ruins, Galilee was a
vibrant land brimming with life. The landscape was full of
trees and groves, mountains and valleys, lakes and seashores.
Even the soil was full of life, making it the perfect place for
a farm, a vineyard, or an olive grove. Along the shores of the
Mediterranean Sea or even along the Sea of Galilee, there
were always fishermen working hard to earn a living.

Compared to the people of Judea who chose to study
and philosophize about religion, the people of Galilee worked
hard. They played pretty hard, too. Galileans were a passionate people—full of life, energy, and enthusiasm for whatever
they were doing. They were not stuck-up, pious, and conser-
vative like their Judean countrymen. No, Galileans would be
much more likely to tell a joke, laugh out loud, speak their
mind, or weep openly than people from Judea, who would
have trained themselves to keep up appearances and control
themselves.

Of course, Galilee was not just a beautiful agricultural
community or fishing village, it was the center of every known
industry and the busy road of the world's commerce. There
were ships coming in from the ports, busy centers of industry
close by, and busy, heavily travelled roads connecting it all.

In fact, one of the great caravan roads of the time, the ancient Via Maris, led right through Nazareth. This meant there were a lot of Gentiles living in or travelling through Nazareth, giving it a sort of international flavor. Although the people of Galilee were still very nationalistic and saw themselves as God's chosen people, there was no room for the intense prejudice against Gentiles that existed in Jerusalem of Judea.

Another difference between Judea and Galilee was the degree of intensity with which they followed Moses' law and rabbinic teaching. In Judea, everything was strictly by the book. The letter of the Law and the additional requirements of rabbinical teaching were followed to the extreme. The people of Galilee were not as legalistic as the people of Jerusalem. It wasn't that they weren't committed to following the teaching of the Old Testament—they were just a little more practical about it.

Edersheim says,

> In regard to religious observances, their practice was simpler…as regarded their Canon-law they often took independent views and generally followed the interpretations of those who tended to the more mild and rational—the more human application of traditionalism.[4]

In practically every way, the people of Galilee were simply more "real" than the people of Judea. They were less pretentious, more in touch with reality and the world around them. They didn't feel the need to put on airs—they were who they were.

Of course, there are two sides to the picture with this type of people. On the one hand, they were more natural, friendlier, warmer, and full of life. On the other hand, these types of people can tend to be more excitable, passionate, and violent. Quite honestly, the Galileans fit both descriptions. From time to time they tended to be more impulsive, straight-spoken, hot-blooded, brave, and intensely national— even to the point of starting riots or making terrorist attempts against Rome. How embarrassing this must have been for the uptight Judeans who would never think of doing such a thing!

So why is it important we know all of this information about Nazareth and the Galilean region?

Simply put, because this is the environment where Jesus spent most of his days on earth. This is where he grew up, where he went to school, where he apprenticed and learned a trade. This is where he lived and worked. These were his people—he was one of them. When we look at what they were like, we learn a lot about him and the life he led.

One of the biggest things we can glean from all of this information is that Jesus lived a real life around very real people. From the stable onward, Jesus didn't make his home among the rich, the influential, the sophisticated, or the powerful. He didn't grow up in Jerusalem—he grew up in Galilee.

He lived among people who knew what it was to work hard.

Jesus lived a very real life around very real people.

He worshipped among those who were intensely committed to following the ways of God and the Old Testament Law, but had little time for the ridiculous legalistic rules attached by the rabbis. He knew practical religion—less rigid, more personal.

Living in Nazareth of Galilee, Jesus came into contact with all types of people—Romans, Greeks, tradesmen, Jews and Gentiles. He interacted with all races in his work as a carpenter. This wouldn't have happened if he'd been born in Jerusalem, but in Nazareth, interacting with Gentiles was normal.

Another thing we can learn from studying the people of Galilee is the type of people with which Jesus was familiar. They certainly weren't the quiet, introspective, sophisticated crowd. No, Jesus was used to being around people who were filled with passion, life, enthusiasm, and emotions. He was comfortable around people who spoke freely, laughed heartily, and lost their temper.

As I'm writing this, I can almost picture Jesus with a big smile on his face, laughing out loud, enjoying himself with his disciples. It also brings to mind the story of Mary and Martha after Lazarus' death, and the fact that Jesus was completely unoffended by their display of uncontrolled emotions.

You see, growing up in Galilee, uncontrolled displays of emotions were normal. People were just people. Although this attitude deeply embarrassed their countrymen to the south, it was this very realism that we see Jesus displaying to everyone he came in contact with during his ministry.

It's funny. No matter who we are or how our circumstances change, a little piece of our hometown always goes with us. For Jesus, this meant he could never have the judgmental, harsh, unfeeling attitude of the Pharisees toward

> *Jesus was open and caring. He treated everyone with equal respect. He was strong when he needed to be strong, and tender when the moment called for it.*

people. In fact, he was just the opposite. Jesus was open and caring. He treated everyone with equal respect. He was strong when he needed to be strong and tender when the moment called for it.

Because of his life in Nazareth, Jesus could feel empathy for the people who came to him. As Hebrews 4:15 says, **"For we do not have a high priest who is unable to empathize with our weaknesses, but we have one who has been tempted in every way, just as we are—yet he did not sin."**

Jesus didn't come to earth surrounded by the beauty of a palace. He didn't grow up among either the politically pampered or the socially elite. No, he lived each day of the first thirty years of his life just like so many of us do. He went through this day-to-day ordinary life, doing the same mundane jobs over and over again.

He loved his family, and on some days, he endured his family. Throughout it all, he took care of and provided for his family, realizing that people are people and that's why we love them. He had friends, and he probably had enemies. He had a business complete with the feeling of accomplishment of a job well done, complaints from clients, competition from rivals, and down times.

The truth is that we don't know much about what happened in the years between the stable and the start of his ministry. One thing we do know is this: he lived. Because he lived a humble life among real people, he could identify with the common man. You and me. The ordinary people who work hard, take care of those we love, and serve God to the best of our ability, day after day. The ones that many would deem "insignificant" were the significant people in his life because he lived a humble life, starting in a stable, then in Nazareth.

Chapter 2 Questions

1. What does learning more about Jesus' hometown, Nazareth, tell you about him?

2. How did this chapter change your mental images of Jesus?

3. Could this new picture of Jesus change your personal relationship with him? How?

4. What nugget of truth did you learn in this chapter?

Chapter 3

Choosing His Team

Do you remember choosing teams in gym class? Two team captains stand in front of the group and choose one by one who they want to be on their teams.

The best athletes were always picked first.

Next were the popular kids. One at a time the choices became fewer, until there were just two kids left. Due to my stellar athletic abilities, I was usually in this group.

Then the dickering began, "You take them."

"No, it's okay, you can have them."

Eventually, someone with an ounce of sensitivity would intervene, choosing sides would end, and the game would start.

As I said before, gym was not my favorite period in the school day. I mean, really, who wants to be picked last?

Of course, it was a different story if we were choosing sides for a Bible quizzing game or a "sword" drill. There I was usually chosen first. When it came to Bible trivia, I was king! (Or queen, but queen doesn't seem to hold the same sense of power!)

The odd thing about the process is that whether I was being picked last in gym class or first for trivia games, it was usually the same people doing the picking. What made me intensely popular one moment and incredibly unwanted the next?

The answer is simple—my ability to help the team win.

Funny how things don't change much as we become adults. Long after we leave the soccer fields and quizzing tournaments behind, we still choose our teams the same way. We look for the most-skilled, best-qualified, uniquely talented individuals that will help us succeed to be on our teams. We want to be associated with the best, the brightest, and the most successful among us. It's the way of the world—the way things get done.

We can be thankful this was not the criteria that Jesus used when he was choosing "his team"—the twelve disciples. When he was looking for twelve individuals that he would spend the next three years teaching, training, and mentoring to carry on his work after he went back to heaven, he didn't go to Jerusalem to search the synagogues for the next great rabbi. He didn't visit Rome to look for a charismatic leader. Instead, he chose for himself twelve men that no one else ever would have expected.

The characteristics they shared weren't their incredible skills or experiences, but rather that each of them carried significant liabilities that would have caused them to be rejected by most other men. But Jesus wasn't like most other men. In each of them he saw something significant—something he could work with. To the most unlikely characters, he extended the invitation, "Come, follow me."

To really understand how incredible his invitation was, we have to look at each man. If you've never studied the biographies of the disciples, you'll be amazed at exactly who these men were that Jesus chose. Let's start with the first disciple Jesus chose:

Andrew

Throughout the Bible, Andrew is most commonly known as "Peter's brother." How ironic, considering it was Andrew that originally encountered Jesus, and then he went to tell Peter about it.

Andrew, Simon Peter's brother, was one of the two who heard what John had said and who had followed Jesus. The first thing Andrew did was to find his brother Simon and tell him, "We have found the Messiah" (that is, the Christ). And he brought him to Jesus (John 1:40–42).

Andrew is one of the most interesting disciples. His name means "manly." He must have been a rough and rugged man (typical in Galilee), the strong, silent type (not typical in Galilee). He grew up on the docks helping his dad with the family fishing business. His best friends were his brother Peter and two other guys, James and John.

They were an odd foursome. Peter, James, and John were your average Galileans—loud and boisterous—never a thought they didn't feel the need to share. Andrew, on the other hand, was more introspective, quiet, and shy.

Because of his personality, Andrew often went unnoticed—except to Jesus. When Jesus met Andrew, he immediately called him as a disciple. As a matter of fact, Andrew was the first disciple Jesus called. **Andrew, Simon Peter's brother, was one of the two who heard what John had said and who had followed Jesus (John 1:40).**

What a surprise this must have been for Andrew! After years of being overshadowed by the overwhelming, overpowering personalities of Peter, James, and John, Jesus chose Andrew. Let's be honest: most people would have picked one of the other guys and allowed them to bring Andrew, the insignificant, quiet one, along. But Jesus chose him—Andrew—the one who didn't stand out in a crowd and didn't have amazing communication skills. Still, Jesus saw something significant in him and said, "Come, follow me."

Peter

If Andrew's liability was his quiet, unassuming personality, Peter's liability was that he went to the polar opposite extreme. (It seems there was no middle ground in this family.)

Peter's personality defined the typical Galilean. He was outspoken, brash, and impulsive. He spoke and acted without thinking. He was intensely passionate—about everything. Even though Peter was not highly educated, he thought he knew everything and shared his knowledge and opinions freely. Although Peter was probably the life of the party at the fishing dock, Jesus was looking for men who would ultimately represent him in Jerusalem and throughout the world. As we see in the Gospels, Peter wasn't exactly known for his diplomacy.

Still, Jesus saw something significant in Peter. Sure, he knew that when they hit Jerusalem the Pharisees and Sadducees would meet Peter and think, "What a Galilean hick!" They'd make fun of his accent and mock his loud-mouth, know-it-all attitudes, but Jesus saw something. He knew that even though the Pharisees would see everything that made Peter insignificant, there was significant potential in Peter. He points out that potential the first time they meet.

Jesus looked at him and said, "You are Simon son of John. You will be called Cephas" (which, when translated, is Peter) (John 1:42).

James

James was one of the first men Jesus called to be one of his disciples.

As Jesus walked beside the Sea of Galilee, he saw Simon and his brother Andrew casting a net into the lake, for they were fishermen. "Come, follow me," Jesus said, "and I will send you out to fish for people." At once they left their nets and followed him.

When he had gone a little farther, he saw James son of Zebedee and his brother John in a boat, preparing their nets. Without delay he called them, and they left their father Zebedee in the boat with the hired men and followed him (Mark 1:16–20).

Like Peter and Andrew, James and John were brothers from Galilee. In fact, Jesus, James, and John were cousins and probably grew up together.

James' father, Zebedee, was an influential man in his community, so James and John were raised in a "well-to-do" family. It would appear James craved the same power and prestige. In fact, that seems to be James' greatest liability—his desperate craving for power. Combine his intense ambition with his impulsive tendencies and quick, violent temper, and it was obvious Jesus would have his hands full if he picked James to be on his team. Still, he called, "James, follow me."

It's not like things got immediately better with James. Throughout the Gospels we see James constantly trying to promote himself to greatness. He, along with his brother, John, was always starting arguments among the disciples about which of them was the most important. James even went as far as getting his mom, Jesus' aunt, to go to her nephew and to get him to promise to make her sons the two most important people in his future kingdom. This didn't go over well with the other disciples, but James didn't care. He wanted to get ahead.

James' ambition superseded his desire to treat people well. One time, Jesus and his disciples were travelling toward a town. When they were not welcomed by the town, James was stunned. How could they reject them?!

Immediately, he got his brother and they both went to Jesus to ask him to call down fire and destroy the town. That's a heart of love and selflessness if I ever saw one! Once again, Jesus had to instruct James that he needed to have a heart of service and compassion for others instead of always trying to advance himself.

Still, no matter how many times James needed to be corrected, Jesus didn't kick him off the team. He kept working with him, seeing something significant among all of these disturbing character traits. Jesus knew someday James would be the man Jesus knew he could be and fulfill the calling God had for his life.

John

John was James' younger brother. Like James, he was raised in a wealthy, influential family. Both men were working with their father, Zebedee, as fishermen when Jesus called them to follow him. Like James, he already knew Jesus because they were cousins.

John shared many of his brother's personality traits. He was ambitious, intolerant, judgmental, critical, condemning of others, and had a very violent temper. Not exactly the personality profile of a minister!

Still, Jesus saw beyond all of this and into John's potential. He saw beyond the cruel, hardened exterior and into the heart of man who would someday be called "the disciple that Jesus loved." While most people would have written John off, Jesus said, "Follow me."

Philip

Philip was a fisherman before Jesus called him to be a disciple.

The next day Jesus decided to leave for Galilee. Finding Philip, he said to him, "Follow Me." Philip, like Andrew and Peter, was from the town of Bethsaida (John 1:43–44).

Philip was not exactly the definition of leadership material. He wasn't the first person you would expect Jesus to choose as a disciple. He was an indecisive man who never faced a decision head on. Instead, he ran from responsibilities and decisions. Either he let the matter slide and refused to deal with it, or he took the situation to someone stronger in character and let them handle it for him. This was a weakness for Philip.

Another weakness is that Philip struggled with having faith. He was more of a worrier. His natural tendency was to look at the situation and see the odds stacked against him. He was a pessimistic man. Everything seemed overwhelming and impossible. Take for example the story told in John 6.

Jesus was in the countryside teaching the people. As the day grew late, Jesus asked his disciples about how to feed the multitude of people. Jesus specifically singled out Philip and asked him what they should do. Jesus was testing Philip to see if he could overcome his pessimistic tendencies. Proving once again that Philip saw the glass as more than half empty, he told Jesus it was impossible to feed that many people—absolutely no way it could happen.

However, Jesus didn't have a pessimist attitude when he looked at Philip. Quite the opposite, he saw Philip's potential. He saw past Philip's tendency to dwell on the negative, but he also saw Philip's willingness to learn. To the pessimistic doubter, he extended the invitation, "Follow me."

Nathanael

Philip found Nathanael and told him, "We have found the one Moses wrote about in the Law, and about whom the prophets also wrote—Jesus of Nazareth, the son of Joseph."

"Nazareth! Can anything good come from there?" Nathanael asked.

"Come and see," said Philip.

When Jesus saw Nathanael approaching, he said of him, "Here truly is an Israelite in whom there is no deceit."

"How do you know me?" Nathanael asked.

Jesus answered, "I saw you while you were still under the fig tree before Philip called you."

Then Nathanael declared, "Rabbi, you are the Son of God; you are the king of Israel."

Jesus said, "You believe because I told you I saw you under the fig tree. You will see greater

things than that." He then added, "Very truly I
tell you, you will see 'heaven open, and the angels
of God ascending and descending on' the Son of
Man" (John 1:45–51).

It would seem when we first meet Nathanael that he is
the only one of the disciples who had no major character
flaws. After all, as soon as Jesus meets him, he pays him a
compliment. Apparently, Nathanael was a man without hypocrisy. He was completely sincere.

He was also very prejudiced, had an issue with judging
others, and was very skeptical. Think about it: his first comment about Jesus was a derogatory comment about Jesus'
hometown!

Nathanael felt he was better than the people of Nazareth.
He looked down on them and judged them through his prejudiced eyes. He never thought the Messiah could come from
such a lowly place.

This superior attitude was going to be a problem in Jesus'
ministry. After all, in the next three years, Jesus' disciples
would come in contact with a Samaritan woman, a demon-
possessed man chained to a headstone, a man with leprosy, a
tax collector, and many more people that weren't quite up to
snuff for Nathanael.

I can almost picture Jesus chuckling as he talks to Nathanael, thinking, "Boy, are the next few years going to be interesting for you!" Still, he didn't allow Nathanael's prejudices
to keep him from experiencing all God had for him. Jesus
knew that in time and through the work of the Holy Spirit,
Nathanael could get over it. From that point on, Nathanael
was on the team.

Matthew

As Jesus went on from there, he saw a man named Matthew sitting at the tax collector's booth. "Follow me," he told him, and Matthew got up and followed him (Matthew 9:9).

Up to this point, the disciples we've studied have possessed personality traits that would have made them unlikely candidates to be chosen by Jesus. However, Matthew had more strikes against him than just a few personality quirks. Before he met Jesus, Matthew made some choices that alienated him from his family, his country, and in the eyes of most people, God.

Matthew grew up in an Israelite family in the town of Galilee. His given name was Levi. He was named after the priestly tribe of Israel. He learned about God and Israel's history as a young child. He had an extensive knowledge of Israelite customs and Bible verses. He should have grown up to be a moral man with great roots in the Israelite faith. However, he made a decision to leave his faith and pursue power and wealth.

Matthew decided to become a Roman tax collector. His career choice made him wealthy and gave him power, but it cost him everything else. Roman tax collectors were hated and seen as traitors. A tax collector's family would disown him. Tax collectors were shunned by the citizens, and Jewish store keepers refused to sell to them. They were banned from entering a synagogue, and they were not allowed to participate in Jewish religious festivals. It was absolutely unthinkable that a religious leader would call Matthew to be a disciple—let alone the Messiah!

Alone and rejected by society, Matthew looked for companionship to the only people he could find acceptance with: prostitutes, thieves, criminals, and other tax collectors. Matthew's life was a wreck. It appeared he had ruined his life. There was absolutely no one who wanted Matthew…except for one person.

One day, Jesus came to Matthew's tax booth. Something about Matthew appealed to Jesus. Jesus asked Matthew to follow him.

Can you imagine the response from the onlookers? The disciples? The religious leaders?

"You asked HIM to be a disciple?"

But Jesus was a strong guy. He stood his ground and not only called Matthew, but actually went to his house for dinner! It was becoming pretty clear that Jesus did not look at people the way the religious leaders did! Jesus rocked everyone's world when he looked beyond Matthew's sinful life and said, "Come, leave it all behind, and follow me."

James, the son of Alphaeus

Now, things are starting to get interesting. If Matthew's call was shocking, then James' call was downright earth shattering. Let's see why.

James' life is one of the most fascinating stories in the entire Bible. Before Jesus called him, James was a member of the Zealots, a violent nationalistic group. The Zealots dreamed of the day when the Jewish people would be free of the Roman's hold over them, and Israel would become the world's dominating power. They did whatever was necessary to achieve this goal.

The Zealots were known to carry daggers in their sleeves. When the opportunity arose to assassinate a Roman, they would quietly work their way close to the official and bury their dagger deep in their victims, killing them. The Zealots were terrorists, murderers, and assassins. James was a Zealot.

Here's where things get more interesting: James and Matthew were brothers. Can you believe it?

Matthew the tax collector/traitor and James the Zealot were brothers!

James despised his brother for being a traitor. Before meeting Jesus, he wouldn't have hesitated to drive his dagger into his brother's heart. The boy he grew up side by side with, the brother he played with, was now his most hated enemy. His hatred must have driven a wedge into the entire family. Family members were forced to choose sides. They were a divided family because of James' hate.

You would think that Jesus could never do anything with such a man. However, nothing could be further from the truth.

Jesus saw something in James that he loved. He called James to be one of his followers. He changed James from the inside out—so much so that James left his Zealot ways and followed Jesus unconditionally. Jesus reconciled James and Matthew to God and to each other. Both men became disciples. They were no longer enemies, but brothers united together preaching the gospel of Jesus Christ together.

Simon the Zealot

Believe it or not, James wasn't the only Zealot Jesus called. Like James, Simon was a member of the Zealots—the radical political party warring to overthrow the Roman government. He was a fierce patriot trained to assassinate and murder on the spot. He was trained in guerilla warfare to burn and plunder villages and towns. He was a reckless person, filled with rage and hatred.

What made Jesus call men like this to follow him? We don't really know. Perhaps he saw beyond their actions and into the passion, loyalty, and perhaps even love for God that caused them to fight so strongly for their beliefs. Whatever he saw, at some point he extended the invitation to Simon to "Put away your weapons of war, and build a heavenly kingdom." From that day onward, Simon was part of the group of men following Jesus.

Thaddeus/Judas (same guy, two names)

Very little is written about this man; he is usually only ever mentioned as "Judas, but not the one who betrayed Jesus." We don't know much about him, except that he, too, was a Zealot. (Not another one!) Being a Zealot, he was an angry, bitter, hateful man. He was a murderer and a terrorist—one of the last men anyone would expect to be chosen as Jesus' disciple. Yet, like the others, Jesus saw something more—something significant. To Judas, he extended the same invitation: "Come, be my disciple."

Thomas

Finally, a disciple who wasn't a Zealot! The truth is that we don't know very much at all about Thomas. We don't know about his family, his

Jesus saw their potential. When he chose them and invested himself into them, he changed their lives.

background, or his occupation. However, the little we do know about him has made him famous!

Thomas struggled with doubt. Although this character trait seems to have plagued his reputation for centuries, it never appears that Jesus criticized Thomas for this quality. Instead, he chose to work with Thomas. He was patient with him, and helped Thomas move from a place of unbelief to become a man of uncompromising faith.

Actually, that's what Jesus did with each and every man that he chose to follow him. Over the course of the three years they spent together, Jesus worked with them. He taught them his ways. He helped them see and overcome their weaknesses, and in many cases, he redirected their weaknesses and turned them into these men's greatest strengths.

It's true. No one else would have gathered this group of men together and said, "These men will change the world." Only Jesus.

Only Jesus saw past their failures, their shortcomings, the things they were lacking, their idiosyncrasies, and their sinful choices. Only Jesus saw their true potential. When he chose them and invested himself into them, he changed their lives.

Not one of the men we've talked about in this chapter stayed the same as he was the day that Jesus called him. Each one was radically changed by spending time with Jesus. They all loved Jesus and followed Jesus even in death. Ultimately, each fulfilled his destiny and played a role in spreading the gospel throughout the world.

The men that most men of their day would have viewed as insignificant rogues became the founding fathers of Christianity—Jesus' apostles.

After Jesus' ascension into heaven, each one played a unique role in spreading the gospel of Christ.

Two of the intense nationalists that wanted to overthrow the Roman government by any means, Simon the Zealot and Thaddeus, became missionaries to Gentile countries.

The traitor/tax-collector-turned-disciple used his extensive knowledge of Old Testament history to write the Gospel of Matthew in an effort to win the Jewish people to Christ.

James the Zealot became the head of the Jerusalem Council until he was martyred.

Philip became an evangelist to Phrygia.

Peter preached boldly, bringing thousands to Christ after Pentecost. He endured prison, beatings, the murder of his wife on the cross before his very eyes, and even his own death upon the cross.

All of them except John were martyred for their commitment to Jesus. Several of them followed in Jesus' footsteps and died by means of crucifixion.

Who could have imagined the potential inside of these men?

Only Jesus.

Who else would have been willing to take a chance on these men with all of their flaws and liabilities?

Only Jesus.

The good news for us is that the same Jesus who saw the raw potential in these men, the clay that simply needed a potter to form them into something useable, is still calling men and women today. He's still searching for the insignificant, the flawed, those who have made wrong choices, and those that no one else would choose. He still calls out, "Come, follow me. Leave it all behind and follow me. Let me remake you into my image. Allow me to completely revolutionize your life. Follow me and see what I can do with a heart that chooses to follow me with complete abandon. Leave your old ways behind and follow me. See what I can do with YOU! I want you on my team."

Chapter 3 Questions

1. Each disciple had his own unique liabilities and strengths. With which disciple did you most closely identify?

2. Which disciple's biography shocked you the most?

3. Which disciple would you be least likely to choose for your team?

4. This chapter teaches that Jesus looks beyond our character and personality deficiencies and sees the potential he can create when we allow him to change us. How does this change the way you see yourself?

5. How does it change the way you look at others?

6. What truths can you apply to your life from this chapter?

Chapter 4

The Samaritans

$\mathcal{R}$oad trip! I love a good road trip! True, I'm not thrilled with the concept of sleeping in strange hotels, but I love travelling to new places, meeting new people, and experiencing new things.

As we take a look into the next vignette of Jesus' life on earth, we meet him with the disciples on a road trip. As required by Jewish law, Jesus and his disciples went to Jerusalem for the Feast of Passover. This is the first Passover he attended after he started his ministry.

From the very beginning, Jesus was a big hit with the religious leaders in Jerusalem. NOT! Look what happened on his first visit to the temple with his disciples.

When it was almost time for the Jewish Passover, Jesus went up to Jerusalem. In the temple courts he found people selling cattle, sheep and doves, and others sitting at tables exchanging money. So he made a whip out of cords, and drove all from the temple courts, both sheep and cattle; he scattered the coins of the money changers and overturned their tables. To those who sold doves

he said, "Get these out of here! Stop turning my Father's house into a market!" (John 2:13-16).

Can you imagine the religious leaders' reaction?

"Who is this guy—this Galilean (remember, his accent gave this fact away)? Who does he think he is to come in here and disturb the way we do things? How dare he say those things about us?"

I can only imagine the shock and anger that surely rose up in the religious leaders and the money changers in the temple.

One thing is for sure: Jesus had not come to Jerusalem to get in good with the religious aristocracy. He wasn't there to make friends and influence people—he was there in obedience to the Law—to worship God. Seeing the current state of the temple, he was completely appalled at the religious leaders' efforts to turn the common man's desire to worship and obey the Law into a commercial venture. In his own way, Jesus was saying, "Who do you think you are to turn God's house into a means of filling your own pockets?"

Before we leave this scene too quickly, we need to really stop and imagine the state of the temple court after Jesus' actions. *Zondervan NIV Bible Commentary Volume 2 New Testament* says,

> *There would have been wild confusion. The animals would be bawling and running about aimlessly; the money changers would be scrambling for coins in the dust and debris on the floor of the court; and the officials would be arguing with Jesus about the rights of the case.*[1]

This was no small scene Jesus had created. More significantly, this was the opening act in the drama that would play out over the next few years between Jesus and the religious leaders in Jerusalem.

Here's the edited version—from the first day they met him, they hated him. He called them out for their religious abuse, and they couldn't wait to get rid of him. That became their mission—ridding Jerusalem of this so-called, self-proclaimed prophet. Let the hostilities commence!

Of course, there was another side of the story to be told in Jesus' trip to Jerusalem—the people. They did not share the views of the religious leaders. Even if only temporarily, they loved him! When they saw the miracles that he performed, his popularity rose quickly.

Now while he was in Jerusalem at the Passover Festival, many people saw the signs he was performing and believed in his name. But Jesus would not entrust himself to them, for he knew all people. He did not need any testimony about mankind, for he knew what was in each person (John 2:23–25).

This only served to make the religious leaders hate him more!

It didn't make them like him anymore when John the Baptist publicly endorsed Jesus during one of his final sermons (John 3:23–36).

As John 4 opens, Jesus and his disciples are leaving Jerusalem and heading back home to Galilee.

Now Jesus learned that the Pharisees had heard that he was gaining and baptizing more disciples than John—although in fact it was not Jesus who baptized, but his disciples. So he left Judea and went back once more to Galilee (John 4:1–3).

Why were Jesus and his disciples on a road trip? Well, they encountered resistance from the religious leaders because they thought his popularity was threatening their authority and power. Because it wasn't yet his time to die, he decided to travel to Galilee to minister. He wasn't running away out of fear; it just wasn't time for him to have the ultimate encounter with the Pharisees, so back to Galilee they travelled!

Now he had to go through Samaria (John 4:4).

To get to Galilee, Jesus and the disciples had to go through Samaria.

So what? Who cares what road they took to get where they were going?

Well, we do! Because even though this seems like a trivial piece of information, it is actually pivotal to understanding Jesus' next encounter. Before we go any further we need to understand that Jews didn't travel through Samaria, because they hated the Samaritans. I mean really, truly, passionately HATED the Samaritans.

Want to know how much they hated Samaritans? All you have to do is look at a map of Israel in the New Testament.

Samaria is located directly between Judea and Galilee.

The shortest route from Jerusalem to Galilee would have been travelling right through Samaria. However, most Jews would never even think of taking that path for fear of being defiled or contaminated by the Samaritans. Instead, they would travel around Samaria. They crossed over the Jordan River, went north until they were well beyond Samaria's northern border, and then crossed back into Galilee—adding many more miles and hours onto the trip. Remember, these people weren't riding in an SUV—they were walking the extra distance. They really hated the Samaritans!

What caused the Jews to hate the Samaritans?

Samaritans mixed the Jewish worship with idol worship. Also, Samaritans aided the enemy and persecuted the Jews when the Jews were trying to rebuild the temple. As decades passed, the hatred and animosity increased until it was common knowledge that Jews didn't even speak to or acknowledge Samaritans.

However, when Jesus was making his journey back home, he went straight through Samaria. I wonder what the religious leaders in Jerusalem would have thought about that?!

So he came to a town in Samaria called Sychar, near the plot of ground Jacob had given to his son Joseph. Jacob's well was there, and Jesus, tired as he was from the journey, sat down by the well. It was about noon (John 4:5–6).

About fifteen miles outside of Samaria was the town of Sychar. Outside of this town was the well where Jesus' ministry to this town took place. It's important to note that this city of Sychar had a rich heritage in biblical times.

Originally, Jacob purchased this piece of land, and Joseph's bones were buried there after they were carried out of Egypt.

The city was in the tribe of Ephraim (Joshua 21:21).

It was here that Joshua assembled the people before his death, and here they renewed their covenant with the Lord (Joshua 24).

After the death of Gideon, it became a place of idolatrous worship, the people worshipping Baal-berith (Judges 9:46).

Later, it was destroyed, but then it was rebuilt, and became the residence of Jeroboam, the king of Israel.

Why does any of this matter to us? It shows us that this city was a place very much like the country we live in today. The inhabitants had a rich religious heritage. Great men had made history there. The entire country of Israel committed itself to following God wholeheartedly on this piece of land.

However, as time went on, they began mingling idol worship with their worship of the one true God. They chose which parts of God they wanted and which parts they didn't want. They claimed the heritage of being from Abraham, but they didn't obey God's laws. They worshipped God the way they felt like it.

This mixture of religion continued into the Babylonian exile. The remnant that was left behind chose to worship idols but mix in a little bit of God's prescribed worship. It became a bizarre mixture of serving God and idols at the same time. They had a lot of religious knowledge and heritage, but they weren't following God. This was the atmosphere of the town Jesus and his disciples were entering.

Jesus and his disciples arrived in this town about noon. Because Jesus was tired, he decided to wait outside of the city by the well while the disciples went to get food. While Jesus was waiting at the well, a woman came to the well to draw water. Being tired and thirsty, he asked her for a drink. This was absolutely not what the woman at the well planned when she began her day.

She expected today to be just like any other day. The same old chores, the same old trip to the well alone. She had no idea that today she had an appointment with God.

When a Samaritan woman came to draw water, Jesus said to her, "Will you give me a drink?" (His disciples had gone into the town to buy food.)

The Samaritan woman said to him, "You are a Jew and I am a Samaritan woman. How can you ask me for a drink?" (For Jews do not associate with Samaritans.) (John 4:7–9).

In New Testament times, it was customary for women to go to the well for water every day. It was a necessity of life. Most of the women went together at the same time, usually in the early morning because it was the coolest part of the day. However, for the woman in our story to go to the well at the normal time of day, she would have to endure the other women.

We all know what that means—especially for a woman with her reputation. Can you imagine how they talked about a woman who had five husbands? The gossip? The innuendos? All over town people knew about this woman and her life.

Obviously, we don't know anything about this woman's childhood or her past, but I wonder which came first, the damage to her soul or her choice to live a life of sin? If she was like most women, her soul was damaged first, and then she chose a promiscuous lifestyle. Of course, her chosen lifestyle only led to more damage in her soul.

The truth is this woman was in hiding. She was hiding from her past, her life, her reputation. She avoided other people and scheduled her life around hiding. That's why she was at the well alone. She was hiding from all the other women who had opinions, comments, and judgments, but no answers. She expected today would be just another day where she went to the well uninterrupted to perform her daily chore in shame. She remembered going to the well with the other women in town, but that was a lifetime ago. Now she went alone—it is easier that way.

As she approached the well, she saw a man sitting there. That man was Jesus. He was waiting for her. It was her day to have a new beginning.

Jesus politely and respectfully asked her for a drink of water. This shocked her. Why would he want a drink from her? He was a Jew and she was a Samaritan. It was common knowledge that she was from a lower class than he was. Still, he asked.

This was only the first of many things that shocked her about Jesus. He treated her with dignity and respect. He listened to her without interrupting her. He wasn't embarrassed to be seen with her. He was genuinely concerned about her as a person.

Jesus didn't look at her the way most men looked at her. He treated her with respect, and not like a woman with a reputation. He didn't treat her like a sexual object, but as a daughter of God. This had to be a new experience for this woman. From the very start, she knew Jesus was different.

Jesus treated her with respect, not like a woman with a reputation.

We have to think this difference caught her off guard. She was used to Jews treating her badly. She was accustomed to men treating her as an object to be used. It was normal to her for "good religious" people to look down on her because of her past and reputation.

I don't think she knew what to do with Jesus. She pointed out to him that they weren't supposed to be talking, but he didn't care.

Completely off her game, she continued to question him.

Jesus answered her, "If you knew the gift of God and who it is that asks you for a drink, you would have asked him and he would have given you living water."

"Sir," the woman said, "You have nothing to draw with and the well is deep. Where can you get this living water? Are you greater than our father Jacob, who gave us the well and drank from it himself, as did also his sons and his livestock?"

Jesus answered, "Everyone who drinks this water will be thirsty again, but whoever drinks the water I give them will never thirst. Indeed, the water I give them will become in them a spring of water welling up to eternal life" (John 4:10–14).

As the conversation went on, she tried to sound as confident as she could. She competently asked him questions. She even pointed out that Jacob, one of Israel's patriarchs, was the Samaritan ancestor as well.

Still, she couldn't help wondering, "Would he be talking to me if he knew who I really am?"

As he spoke, his words pierced through the calluses on her heart. When he offered her a chance to avoid going to that well every day, she leaped at the offer. It would be great to be free from that shameful experience. Can you imagine? No more coming to the well in the heat of the day. No more dealing with those awful women!

The woman said to him, "Sir, give me this water so that I won't get thirsty and have to keep coming here to draw water" (John 4:15).

There was no way she was going to miss an opportunity like this!

Then the other shoe dropped.

He told her, "Go, call your husband and come back" (John 4:16).

He wanted to meet her husband. What would he think if she told him the truth? Would he turn away like all the others? Would he be repulsed that he had spoken to her? Why did he have to go there?

She sheepishly answered, "I have no husband."

Jesus said, "I know," and then told her the story of her life.

59

Jesus said to her, "You are right when you say you have no husband. The fact is, you have had five husbands, and the man you now have is not your husband. What you have just said is quite true" (John 4:17–18).

Jesus knew that before this woman could start a new life, she needed to stop hiding from her old life. She had to stop running from her past before she could ever have a future. Because Jesus knew this, he brought the truth right out into the open.

Before she could start a new life, she needed to stop hiding from her old life. She had to stop running from her past before she could ever have a future!

It's important to notice in verses 17–18 that Jesus' offer of a new life didn't change when he found out the dark secrets of her life.

Why? Because he already knew everything about her. Although he didn't condone her lifestyle, he didn't condemn her as a hopeless case or chime in with those who hated her. Instead, he saw her as a precious child of God, and he offered her a way out of her life of sin and into a new life as a daughter of God. Ultimately, this woman experienced a change in her own life, and she became a catalyst for change in her whole community. Verses 39–41 tell us that many in her community became believers because she brought them to Jesus.

You know what's interesting? That's what Jesus saw the first time he saw her. Yes, he saw a Samaritan, and a woman with a damaged soul who made sinful choices in her life. But he also saw a woman who was looking for a change, and he knew he had the power to give her that change. Finally, he saw the enormous potential she had and the purpose he had for her in his kingdom.

That's what God sees when he looks at each of us. He sees everything. Everything we've been through, everything we've done, and everything we can become. He says, "If she'll go along with my plan for her life, her life will be amazing!"

God doesn't think you're stupid or useless or beyond hope. He sees inside of you enormous potential that he can use in this life and throughout eternity.

But the story doesn't end there. Let's see what happens next.

Well, if Jesus and his behavior made her uncomfortable, the fact that he knew everything about her made her really uncomfortable.

How could he know everything about her?

Obviously, he was a prophet.

What do you do when you're confronted with a prophet? Sound as religious as possible!

> **"Sir," the woman said, "I can see that you are a prophet. Our ancestors worshiped on this mountain, but you Jews claim that the place where we must worship is in Jerusalem."**
>
> **"Woman," Jesus replied, "believe me, a time is coming when you will worship the Father neither on this mountain nor in Jerusalem. You Samaritans worship what you do not know; we worship what we do know, for salvation is from the Jews. Yet a time is coming and has now come when the true worshipers will worship the Father in**

the Spirit and in truth, for they are the kind of worshipers the Father seeks. God is spirit and His worshipers must worship in the Spirit and in truth."

The woman said, "I know that Messiah" (called Christ) "is coming. When he comes, he will explain everything to us."

Then Jesus declared, "I, the one speaking to you—I am he" (John 4:19–26).

Rather than dealing with the truth about her life, this woman tried to hide behind religious discussions and questions. This should keep him from talking about her true identity.

It did. Instead, he told her about *his* true identity when he introduced himself as the Messiah. This was the first and only time that Jesus declared himself as the Messiah until he was on trial the night before his crucifixion. I find it amazing that he didn't make this significant statement in the temple, to a religious leader, or even to a Jew. Instead, he told a Samaritan woman with a bad reputation. With that statement, he spoke hope, life, purpose, and significance into her life.

That was the end of the conversation between Jesus and the woman at the well, because the disciples interrupted when they came back with the food.

Just then his disciples returned and were surprised to find him talking with a woman. But no one asked, "What do you want?" or "Why are you talking with her?" (John 4:27).

Just because the conversation ended didn't mean the story did. John 4:28–29 shows us that when Jesus revealed he was the Messiah, this woman believed him. Her belief led her to do the most amazing thing:

Then, leaving her water jar, the woman went back to the town and said to the people, "Come, see a man who told me everything I ever did. Could this be the Messiah?"

Her encounter with Jesus changed her. Remember, when she first went to the well, it was because she was hiding. She was trying to avoid the townspeople and everything they knew about her and her past. However, after spending time with Jesus, she actually went into the town and told all the people that the Messiah had come and told her everything she ever did. Because she met Jesus and he accepted her, because he offered her not only eternal life but a new life here on earth, she didn't have to hide anymore. Her former shame became her testimony.

Verses 39–42 show us the tremendous results of this woman's testimony.

Many of the Samaritans from that town believed in him because of the woman's testimony, "He told me everything I ever did."

So when the Samaritans came to him, they urged him to stay with them, and he stayed two days. And because of his words many more became believers.

They said to the woman, "We no longer believe just because of what you said; now we have heard for ourselves, and we know that this man really is the Savior of the world."

Because she was willing to share her testimony, including acknowledging her past, many of the Samaritans in her town went to Jesus and believed in him as well. Even the women who judged the Samaritan women so harshly rushed to meet Jesus and believe in him when they heard her story. Why?

Because it wasn't just the woman at the well who needed Jesus. She wasn't the only one with a damaged soul and a damaged life. Jesus offered the same thing to everyone in the town—a new life.

However, before we rush off too quickly to celebrate this woman's new life and her happy ending, there's something we need to stop and focus on. According to these Scriptures, after hearing the woman's testimony about Jesus, the people of the town invited Jesus to stay for *two days* and teach them.

Think about the irony of it: on his way out of Jerusalem (because of the religious leaders' jealousy and hatred) Jesus stops and holds a revival meeting in Sychar of Samaria! While most good Jews wouldn't even think of talking to these people, Jesus and the disciples stop, stay overnight, and hold a mass evangelistic crusade!

This was unthinkable!

That's what made Jesus amazing. He not only looked past the label of "woman of ill repute" to minister to the woman at the well. He looked beyond the prejudice and the hatred toward the Samaritans and offered salvation to them. As a result, many more from that town became believers.

As I read this biblical account of Jesus' time with the Samaritans, I can't help but remember a story he told later on in his ministry. Ironically, this story was told in response to a question from one of the Jewish teachers of the Law.

In reply Jesus said: "A man was going down from Jerusalem to Jericho, when he was attacked by robbers. They stripped him of his clothes, beat him and went away, leaving him half dead.

A priest happened to be going down the same road, and when he saw the man, he passed by on the other side.

> So too, a Levite, when he came to the place and saw him, passed by on the other side.
>
> But a Samaritan, as he traveled, came where the man was; and when he saw him, he took pity on him. He went to him and bandaged his wounds, pouring on oil and wine. Then he put the man on his own donkey, brought him to an inn and took care of him. The next day he took out two denarii and gave them to the innkeeper. 'Look after him,' he said, 'and when I return, I will reimburse you for any extra expense you may have.'" (Luke 10:30–35).

As I read this story, I can't help but think of how Jesus was truly the Good Samaritan to the people in the town of Sychar. When he saw a woman who was bleeding and dying spiritually, he couldn't just walk past. He stopped, ministered to her, and spoke words of life that ultimately brought healing to her soul.

When he was asked to stay and minister to the whole town, he couldn't be like the priest or the Levite and say, "Sorry, I can't stay here—this is a Samaritan town." Instead, he stayed and brought the message of the Messiah to anyone and everyone in that town who wanted to listen.

That's the God we serve—a God who looks beyond labels, social barriers, and prejudices of all kinds and says, **"Everyone who calls on the name of the Lord will be saved" (Romans 10:13).**

Here's one last interesting fact about Jesus' ministry in Samaria. I learned this from John MacArthur's book, *Twelve Extraordinary Women.* He says,

> *Within three years after the Samaritan woman's meeting with Christ at Jacob's well, the church was founded.*

Its influence quickly spread from Jerusalem into all Judea, and Samaria, and from there to the uttermost parts of the earth....This meant the Samaritan woman and the men of her city would soon be able to find fellowship and teaching in a context where there was neither Hebrew nor Samaritan, Jew nor Greek, slave nor free, male nor female; but where all were one in Christ Jesus (Gal. 3:28)[2]

What a dramatic difference Jesus made! Because of his life, death, and resurrection, a woman most would have written off as too sinful to be saved, a town that most would have shunned, in an area that was hated and avoided at all costs, was offered salvation, a fresh start, and the opportunity to become a part of the community of believers.

Today, the same Jesus is waiting for each of us, offering us the same opportunity. No matter who you are or what you've been through in life, God already knows. He offers you a new life. He wants to forgive your sins and heal you from your past. He longs to heal you from the heartache you have experienced throughout your life and deliver you from generational sins that were passed down to you from your family. He wants to give you a new life and teach you new ways of thinking, talking, and living.

It doesn't matter what your past or background. Jesus doesn't have a pile of good people that he can work with and a pile of other people who are too damaged to help. To Jesus, we are all damaged. We all come with problems and emotional baggage and generational sins. Even the women who judged the Samaritan woman so harshly had their own damage. That's why they rushed to meet Jesus and believe in him when they heard the Samaritan woman's story.

Like he did with the woman at the well, Jesus wants to have an appointment with you. He already knows everything about your past, your heart, and your soul. He is offering you the chance to be healed, start over, and become new. All you have to do is tell Jesus you want him and then cooperate with him as he works to change your life. Like he waited for the woman at the well, Jesus is waiting for you. The choice is yours: Will you accept his offer of a new life?

Chapter 4 Questions

1. What does it tell you about Jesus that he chose to go through Samaria rather than around it?

2. Can you identify with the Samaritan woman's desire to avoid people and hide rather than face people's opinions, comments, and judgments?

3. What things in your life—past or present—are causing you to hide in shame?

4. Describe some ways that modern women hide behind religion like the Samaritan woman did with Jesus.

5. What does the fact that Jesus chose to reveal his identity as the Messiah to a Samaritan woman with a bad reputation say about Jesus' heart and mission? What does this mean to you?

6. Has your life ever been changed by someone's willingness to overcome her shame and share her testimony?

Chapter 5

Foreigners

Prejudice.

Hate.

Racism.

Segregation.

*A*ll of these and more were very prominent among the Jews when Jesus walked the earth. For even though Judaism was divided and there wasn't much love lost between the inhabitants of Judea and the residents of Galilee, there was one thing they could both wholeheartedly agree on. They all hated foreigners. The rude Galileans were as "patriotic" as the ceremonious Pharisees.

Unfortunately, the Jews were surrounded by foreigners because Rome was in power. Rome controlled everything: the government, the taxes, the laws, and even to a point, Rome had its nose in temple business. The Jews despised the Roman occupation. They resented foreigners reigning over them, the chosen people of God.

It wasn't just Romans the Jews hated. As descendants of Abraham, and as God's chosen people, they felt it was their responsibility to separate themselves from outsiders. Rather than being a light that attracted the Gentiles to God, the Jews chose to stay away from the Gentiles, fearing they might become corrupted. This wasn't what God intended, but it was the result of generations of Israelites compromising with their Gentile neighbors, falling into sin and idolatry, and suffering the consequences. After the Babylonian captivity, the Jews were tired of being punished for their compromise, and decided it was best to avoid contact with Gentiles all together.

It's an unfortunate thing that the Jews got things so mixed up. True, God intended for the people of Israel to be his holy people, set apart for him, living by his ways and following his laws. Ideally, their commitment to him would have been so strong that they would never have fallen into the trap of idolatry, and that their way of life would have attracted the Gentile world to him. It was God's will that they influence the Gentile world rather than the Gentile world always being a poor influence on them. We know from history that isn't what happened. Each and every time, the people of God were influenced by the people of the world instead of vice versa. In an effort to end the cycle, the Jewish people chose to stay as separate and unattached from the Gentile world as possible. Here are some examples:

Entering the house of a heathen caused you to be defiled until morning (John 18:28).

It was against the law for Jews to visit with or associate with a Gentile (Acts 10:28).

No pious Jew would sit down and eat at the table of a Gentile (Acts 11:1–3).

All of these rules are what makes the next few portions of Scripture we are going to look at so fascinating. If you thought Jesus turned heads when he held revival meetings in

Samaria, can you imagine the response he got when he actually performed miracles for Gentiles?

Hang onto your hats as we look at a few examples of Jesus ministering to foreigners!

Let's start with Matthew 8:5–13 and the story of the centurion with the sick servant.

> **When Jesus had entered Capernaum, a centurion came to him, asking for help.**
>
> **"Lord," he said, "my servant lies at home paralyzed, suffering terribly."**
>
> **Jesus said to him, "Shall I come and heal him?"**
>
> **The centurion replied, "Lord, I do not deserve to have you come under my roof. But just say the word, and my servant will be healed. For I myself am a man under authority, with soldiers under me. I tell this one, 'Go,' and he goes; and that one, 'Come,' and he comes. I say to my servant, 'Do this,' and he does it."**
>
> **When Jesus heard this, he was amazed and said to those following him, "Truly I tell you, I have not found anyone in Israel with such great faith. I say to you that many will come from the east and the west, and will take their places at the feast with Abraham, Isaac and Jacob in the kingdom of heaven. But the subjects of the kingdom will be thrown outside, into the darkness, where there will be weeping and gnashing of teeth."**
>
> **Then Jesus said to the centurion, "Go! Let it be done just as you believed it would." And his servant was healed at that moment.**

Finding Significance

This is an amazing story—for more reasons than one. It is certainly more than just an account of a miraculous event. It is one of the first scenes where we see Jesus living out God's original plans for his people as he ministers to the needs of a Gentile. Albert Barnes points out in his commentary *Barnes Notes on the New Testament* that in this scene, we see the first glimpses of Simeon's prophecy being fulfilled, **"For my eyes have seen your salvation, which you have prepared in the sight of all nations: a light for revelation to the Gentiles, and the glory of your people Israel" (Luke 2:30–32).**

Still, this man who came to Jesus wasn't just any Gentile, he was a centurion. A centurion was a Roman military officer who commanded one hundred men. Barnes says that he was probably commander-in-chief of part of the Roman army, which was quartered at Capernaum, and kept garrison there.

Remember, as much as the Jews hate foreigners, they really hate the Roman army—specifically the garrison that kept a watchful eye on the towns in Galilee. Here was the head of the garrison, coming to ask Jesus for help!

Can't you just see all the former Zealots-turned-apostles waiting to see what Jesus would do when this man approached?

Think about it. Not too long ago, these guys would have taken this opportunity of being so close to the centurion to slip a dagger into his heart. Now he's asking for their leader's help?!

Look at Jesus' response: **Jesus said to him, "Shall I come and heal him?"**

Are you kidding me? Jesus is offering to go to this guy's house? Doesn't he know that it's against Jewish law to go to a Gentile's house? Plus, it isn't going to make you overly

72

popular if you're going to visit the head of the local Roman garrison! Forget the former Zealots; all of the disciples must have held their breath, thinking, "Are we really going to his house?" as they waited for the centurion to answer.

Thankfully, they could all breathe a sigh of relief when the centurion said, **"Lord, I do not deserve to have you come under my roof. But just say the word, and my servant will be healed."**

But let's be honest—the centurion was familiar with the area. He knew Jewish law. He knew that if Jesus went to his house, Jesus would have been deemed ceremonially defiled. Out of kindness, the centurion said, "No, you don't have to come." Some suggest the centurion felt unworthy of having Jesus suffer such an inconvenience for his sake.

Others say the centurion's words have nothing to do with such concerns, but rather that the centurion felt unworthy in the face of Jesus' authority. He, as a soldier, understood the chain of command and the definition of authority. He knew all Jesus had to do was command that his servant be healed, and it would be done.

That's when Jesus turned to those who were following him (the Jews, including the disciples) and paid this Gentile soldier an outstanding compliment. He said, **"Truly I tell you, I have not found anyone in Israel with such great faith. I say to you that many will come from the east and the west, and will take their places at the feast with Abraham, Isaac and Jacob in the kingdom of heaven. But the subjects of the kingdom will be thrown outside, into the darkness, where there will be weeping and gnashing of teeth."**

Then everyone's jaws dropped! What was he saying? This was revolutionary!

These verses are more than just Jesus complimenting this man on his incredible faith (which by the way, did show more understanding of Jesus' authority under God than most Jews could comprehend). It actually speaks of the end times when people will be gathered from the four corners of the globe for the future Messianic banquet.

To fully grasp how revolutionary this teaching was, you need to understand that the Jews were familiar with the concept of the Messianic banquet. It came from Old Testament prophecies like Isaiah 25:6–8 **"On this mountain the Lord Almighty will prepare a feast of rich food for all peoples, a banquet of aged wine—the best of meats and the finest of wines. On this mountain he will destroy the shroud that enfolds all peoples, the sheet that covers all nations; he will swallow up death forever. The Sovereign Lord will wipe away the tears from all faces; he will remove his people's disgrace from all the earth. The Lord has spoken."**

The Jews loved this teaching. They longed for the day when this promise would be fulfilled.

Unfortunately, they didn't totally understand it. Over the years, the rabbis taught that this prophecy was about a "Jews Only" banquet with a big "No Gentiles Allowed" sign on the door. Now, Jesus is saying that not all of the Jews are getting into the banquet! You're not invited based on your genealogy, but on whether or not you have faith in Jesus.

Then he said something even more shocking: There would be Gentiles at the banquet—lots of them!

This entire concept was unheard of to the Jews. It was shocking, surprising, and appalling. It rocked their world.

Fortunately, it didn't rock God's world at all, because this had been his intention from the very beginning. It was always his design that ALL men come to him. His purpose in creating the Jewish nation was that they would draw all men to him. It was never God's design to take all the Jews to heaven and send all the Gentiles to hell. As Jesus spoke to the centurion, he was introducing them to the concept of the Great Commission for the first time.

Then he spoke the word and the centurion's servant was healed.

This happened near the beginning of Jesus' ministry. Let's fast-forward and see other encounters Jesus had with foreigners.

Jesus left that place and went to the vicinity of Tyre. He entered a house and did not want anyone to know it; yet he could not keep his presence secret (Mark 7:24).

Another day, another debate with the religious leaders—this had become a pattern in Jesus' life. At the beginning of our next passage of Scripture, it appears that Jesus had had enough of this cycle. He needed a break. So he left and went to Tyre, to get some rest and a little bit of privacy. All of the commentaries stress that he did not go there for public ministry. Still, people in need found him.

In fact, as soon as she heard about him, a woman whose little daughter was possessed by an impure spirit came and fell at his feet. The woman was a Greek, born in Syrian Phoenicia. She begged Jesus to drive the demon out of her daughter (Mark 7:25–26).

If you've ever loved someone who was in desperate need of help that you couldn't provide, then you can identify with this woman. As any mother with a sick child will tell you, you don't care what it takes; you're going to get help for your child. When this woman came to Jesus, she had a one-track mind.

She didn't care that he was a Jew and she was a Gentile. She didn't even care that he was tired. Her child was in desperate need of help and she was going to do whatever it took to get help. When she heard that Jesus was in town, she immediately went to him and begged "Please, help my daughter!"

At first read, Jesus' reply seems a little cruel. **"First let the children eat all they want," he told her, "for it is not right to take the children's bread and toss it to the dogs" (Mark 7:27).**

A little cold, don't you think? However, upon further investigation we find it isn't as bad as it initially sounds.

In his book *One Perfect Life*, John MacArthur says the term "dogs" isn't the derogatory term describing a mangy, vicious mongrel that the Jews usually used when they were referring to the Gentiles. Instead, Jesus used a word that would be interpreted "household pet," an animal that had a place in the household, but not the prominent place that children had. In short, Jesus was saying, "It's not time for the ministry to the Gentiles to begin." His first responsibility was to preach to the children of Israel. The time for the Gentiles would come later.

Still, this woman didn't care about Jewish-Gentile relations. She was a mommy and her little girl needed help NOW. So she continued, **"Lord," she replied, "even the dogs under the table eat the children's crumbs" (Mark 7:28).**

This was one tenacious lady! She needed what Jesus had to give, and she was going to get it. True, she knew she wasn't worthy. She acknowledged she wasn't a Jew. But like the centurion before her, she seemed to have an understanding of God's love and mercy toward all of mankind that led her to continue humbly begging for her need to be met.

Seeing her tremendous faith in the God who could do anything and loved everybody, Jesus fulfilled her request.

Then he told her, "For such a reply, you may go; the demon has left your daughter." She went home and found her child lying on the bed, and the demon gone (Mark 7:29–30).

Well, word was out that Jesus was in town and it was time for him to hit the road again.

Then Jesus left the vicinity of Tyre and went through Sidon, down to the Sea of Galilee and into the region of the Decapolis (Mark 7:31).

The Decapolis was a confederation of ten Hellenized cities south of Galilee and mostly east of the Jordan River. The district containing ten cities was rebuilt, colonized, and granted special privileges by Rome in 65 BC to preserve Greek culture in the region. Most of the people who lived in these cities were Gentiles.

Again, Jesus didn't go to these cities to minister, but to get some rest. Still, those who were in need found him, and he could not turn them away.

There some people brought to him a man who was deaf and could hardly talk, and they begged Jesus to place his hand on him.

After he took him aside, away from the crowd, Jesus put his fingers into the man's ears. Then he spit and touched the man's tongue.

He looked up to heaven and with a deep sigh said to him, "Ephphatha!" (which means "Be opened!").

At this, the man's ears were opened, his tongue was loosened and he began to speak plainly.

Jesus commanded them not to tell anyone. But the more he did so, the more they kept talking about it. People were overwhelmed with amazement. "He has done everything well," they said. "He even makes the deaf hear and the mute speak" (Mark 7:32–37).

Once again we see Jesus fulfilling God's original plan for the children of Israel, and being a light that attracted the Gentiles to God. As with the Syrophoenecian woman, Jesus didn't come to town to minister, but to rest. Once again, people who were in desperate need came to him begging for help. Because of his great love for people, he could not turn them away. He took the man aside privately and healed him.

Then Jesus made a request from the man and his friends. He commanded them not to tell anyone.

Naturally, they couldn't listen. There are just some things you can't keep to yourself without bursting. Being able to hear and speak after years of hearing and saying nothing was just too big of a secret. It had to be shared.

As it was shared, people were drawn to Christ. The phrase they used was, **"He does everything well."** With that, his hours of seclusion were over and he was thrust into the crowds. People were seeking him out, wanting to hear what he had to say and see the miraculous things he could do. As we see in Mark 8, the Gentiles were drawn to him.

During those days another large crowd gathered. Since they had nothing to eat, Jesus called his disciples to him and said, "I have compassion for these people; they have already been with me three days and have nothing to eat. If I send them home hungry, they will collapse on the way, because some of them have come a long distance" (Mark 8:1–3).

True confession time: I have studied the Bible for many years. However, it wasn't until I was doing the research for this chapter that I realized that the feeding of the four thousand took place in Gentile territory. (Okay, yes, I am a little embarrassed.) I mean, I knew there were two mass feedings—one where Jesus fed five thousand people and another where Jesus fed four thousand people. Still, I never realized that the first time he fed Jews, while the second time he fed the Gentiles. Yet Scripture shows that Jesus was still in the region of the Decapolis when this miracle occurred.

Apparently, word spread like wildfire that Jesus had healed the deaf man. The Scripture says a large crowd gathered around him, and they stayed for three days! That's a long time to go without food! Compare this to the feeding of the five thousand, where the crowd gathered, ate, and left in one day, and you can see how dedicated and eager these people were to hear Jesus' teaching and experience his healings.

Notice that it was Jesus who pointed out that these people needed to eat. He said to his disciples, **"I have compassion for these people; they have already been with me three days and have nothing to eat. If I send them home hungry, they will collapse on the way, because some of them have come a long distance."**

I love the way he says that—I have compassion for these people. Yes, at this moment he was referring to the fact that he could identify with their need for food. Remember, Jesus was in a human body—he was probably hungry, too. Still, we see in this whole story Jesus' compassion reached out to more than just their physical needs. It was his compassion, his love for all of mankind, that led him to minister to them for three days in the first place.

He didn't have to do it. He could have said, "I'm too tired, go away," but instead he spent three days ministering to them.

He didn't have to heal their sick. He could have reminded them of their position as Gentiles and refused their requests. Certainly, the religious leaders would have.

He didn't have to feed them. After all, he was a Jew and Jews didn't eat with Gentiles. He could have used this as a technicality and said after the first day, "Go home and feed yourselves." But he chose another course.

He chose compassion. He took pity on their physical and spiritual needs and he fed both. For three days, he ministered to their souls before he performed the incredible miracle of providing them with food. Then, seeing their commitment and dedication, he performed a miracle that the Jews had certainly thought would be exclusive to them.

He told the crowd to sit down on the ground. When he had taken the seven loaves and given thanks, he broke them and gave them to his disciples to distribute to the people, and they did so. They had a few small fish as well; he gave thanks for them also and told the disciples to distribute them. The people ate and were satisfied. Afterward, the disciples picked up seven basketfuls of broken pieces that were left over. About four thousand were present. After he had sent them away, he got into the boat with his disciples and went to the region of Dalmanutha (Mark 8:6–10).

Over four thousand men ate that day. Some scholars say when you add in women and children there were probably at least sixteen thousand people in that crowd. Before we get too caught up in how many people were physically fed, we need to remember how many were spiritually fed in the three days leading up to the miracle. How many people heard Jesus talk about the kingdom of God? How many were healed or delivered? These numbers aren't recorded in the Bible, but it's safe to assume if sixteen thousand stayed to the end, there were probably at least twenty thousand people who heard what he had to say over the course of the three days.

These people, mostly foreigners living in a Gentile region, had an encounter with the Messiah. I wonder how many, when they were presented with the news of the gospel just a few short years later, said, "Yeah, I remember him. I heard him teach. I was part of the crowd he fed. There was something very powerful about him."

We don't know what spiritual foundation was laid in the lives of people who experienced a Jew that didn't treat them with contempt, hatred, or prejudice, but instead saw them through the eyes of compassion. A Jew who loved them like God did, saw their value as human souls, and taught them spiritual truths of the kingdom of God.

He was a revolutionary—very different from the other men of his time. He wasn't motivated by hate, prejudice, or fear of being contaminated. Even though he knew it was God's plan to first introduce the promised Messiah to the Jews, he also knew in God's ultimate plan, when he was lifted up from the earth, he would draw all people to himself (John 12:32). He knew the Great Marriage Supper of the Lamb would include people of every tongue, tribe, race, and nation. That was God's plan all along.

Personal Application

A few years ago, I was talking to a friend of mine about a trip we were planning. The conversation took an unexpected turn when I started to hear fear in her voice. She was getting up the nerve to ask a question that was weighing on her mind. Finally she said, "Do they know I'm Hispanic?"

Honestly, her question caught me off guard. I never thought about this being an issue. However, as I listened to her tell me about times when it *was* an issue, my heart broke. I thought, "How could anyone see my friend as anything but a beautiful woman of God?" Although I couldn't relate to what she was feeling, her fears, brought on by past experiences, were very real. She knew what it felt like to experience prejudice and racism.

After we talked, I began recalling instances where I've seen people's prejudice in action. I remember hearing a so-called "godly Christian man" make racial comments about a missionary of another ethnicity. I cringed when I heard it, and I still shudder when I think about it. What kind of people could harbor such feelings in their heart and still call themselves religious? I guess you could ask that same question of the Pharisees.

Of course, not all prejudice is racially motivated. Perhaps you've experienced prejudice based on your age, your gender, your size, or your economic level. Maybe as you've

> Never be ashamed of being yourself and never let anyone attach shame to you.

82

been reading these verses about the Gentiles, you can identify because you know what it feels like to be discriminated
against, hated, or treated as insignificant because of prejudice.

If this is you, let me first say that I am so deeply sorry. No
one should ever be treated badly simply for being who God
created them to be. Never be ashamed of being yourself and
never let anyone attach shame to you. You are God's precious
daughter, created in his image for the distinct purpose he
has designed for your life. No one has the right to attach any
other label to you. In Christ, you are free to be exactly who
he created you to be.

If you are carrying around the burdens and wounds of
another person's hatred and prejudice, I encourage you to be
like the Gentiles in these Scriptures and tenaciously beg Jesus
for healing. Just as he met both physical and spiritual needs in
the New Testament, he is available to heal both physical and
spiritual wounds today.

It is his greatest desire to heal the parts of your soul
that have been wounded by the words and actions of other
people. He wants to take away the pain, remove their poison,
and help you to see yourself through his eyes. He wants to
remove any labels of insignificance they may have placed on
you, and speak words of significance, hope, and promise into
your life. Come to him today and allow the God who is free
from all forms of prejudice, hate, contempt, or discrimination
to heal your heart and fill you with his acceptance and his joy.
Then you, like the Gentiles who experienced Jesus' healing
here on earth, can share your testimony with others who will
say, **"He has done everything well."**

Chapter 5 Questions

1. Have you ever been the victim of racism or prejudice?

2. Have you ever avoided people because of preconceived ideas, racism, or prejudice?

3. How can we, as followers of Jesus, avoid adopting the Jews' attitude toward those who are different than us in today's culture?

4. How can we fulfill the Great Commission and influence the world around us without being corrupted by the sin all around us?

5. What are some specific behavioral patterns of Jesus' that will help us overcome prejudice and show God's love to all people?

6. How did the chapter help you see yourself differently?

Chapter 6

The Unclean

"Unclean! Unclean!"

*T*he odds were that you would probably hear a leper announcing his arrival before you actually saw him.

"Unclean! Unclean!"

These words were the symbol of grief and isolation.

Once you heard those words, you could be sure that a leper would be following soon. Before long, you'd see him, looking like he was in mourning with his clothes torn, his hair a mess, and the lower part of his face and upper lip covered. His entire appearance was meant to show those who didn't already hear that he was unclean and should be avoided.

It started off as a safety precaution. The original intention was to protect the community of Israelites from disease as they travelled through the desert—a means of avoiding a widespread epidemic.

Anyone with such a defiling disease must wear torn clothes, let their hair be unkempt, cover the lower part of their face and cry out, 'Unclean! Unclean!' As long as they have the disease they

remain unclean. They must live alone; they must live outside the camp (Leviticus 13:45–46).

In New Testament times, lepers were to be kept isolated from everyone except other lepers. They were not allowed to enter the temple or Jerusalem, or any walled city. It was a hard, lonely life. Anyone with leprosy had to endure not only the symptoms of the disease, but also the pain of loneliness as they were separated from their family and friends and anything connected with their normal lives.

In true form, Rabbinic law only served to make the plight of the leper more unbearable. Edersheim says,

> *The Mishnic section about 'clean and unclean' was the largest and most intricate in the Rabbinic code... In the elaborate code of defilements, leprosy was not only one of the 'fathers of uncleanness', but next to defilement from the dead, stood foremost among them. Not merely actual contact with the leper, but even his entrance defiled a habitation, and everything in it, to the beams on the roof.*
>
> *But beyond this, Rabbinic harshness or fear carried its provisions to the utmost sequences of unbending logic...Rabbinism loved to trace disease to moral causes....Thus, childlessness and leprosy are described as chastisements, which indeed procure for the sufferer forgiveness of sins, but cannot, like other chastisements, be regarded as the outcome of love, nor be received in love.[1]*

Don't you just love the Jewish rabbis that enforced the Law? Sure, they might have understood every nuance in the Levitical system, but they completely missed the heart and intent of the God who gave the Law. These men were the epitome of the heartless know-it-alls described in 1 Corinthians 13:1–3, **"If I speak in the tongues of men or of angels, but do not have love, I am only a resounding gong or a clanging cymbal. If I have the gift of prophecy and can fathom all mysteries and all knowledge, and if I have a faith that can move mountains, but do not have love, I am nothing. If I give all I possess to the poor and give over my body to hardship that I may boast, but do not have love, I gain nothing."**

Trust me, these men didn't see themselves as nothing! They viewed themselves as the guardians of the keys to the kingdom of God, the preservers of holiness in Israel.

Jesus, on the other hand, described them more accurately when he said, **"Woe to you, teachers of the law and Pharisees, you hypocrites! You are like whitewashed tombs, which look beautiful on the outside, but on the inside are full of the bones of the dead and everything unclean. In the same way, on the outside you appear to people as righteous, but on the inside you are full of hypocrisy and wickedness"** (Matthew 23:27–28).

Because the rabbis felt that leprosy was a punishment for sins, they didn't have compassion on those with leprosy. Instead, they increased their burdens to make them feel greater punishment. Another rabbi boasted that he threw stones at them to keep them far off, while others hid themselves or ran away.

Can you imagine how the heart of God wept at the cruel, inhumane treatment given to a sick, suffering person by those who claimed to be his representatives?

Contrast this to Jesus and his response when confronted with a leper. The account is found in Matthew, Mark, and Luke, but we're going to focus on Dr. Luke's account.

While Jesus was in one of the towns, a man came along who was covered with leprosy. When he saw Jesus, he fell with his face to the ground and begged him, "Lord, if you are willing, you can make me clean" (Luke 5:12).

Jesus was with his disciples in one of the towns in Galilee when they encountered a leper. Notice that Luke, a physician, says the man was covered in leprosy, perhaps indicating his was an extremely serious case.

Before we go into Jesus' response, let's ask ourselves, what would a religious leader have done in this position?

As we said before, history tells us that a religious leader would have run away and done all he could to avoid the man, even going to extremes.

That isn't the route Jesus took. Instead, Jesus allowed the man to come close to him. Jesus allowed the man to speak to him and ask him, **"Lord, if you are willing, you can make me clean."**

Apparently, the man with leprosy had no doubt that Jesus *could* heal him. The question was, *would* he heal him? After all, the other religious leaders of this day *couldn't* and more importantly, *wouldn't* if they could. They carried the attitude "You sinned, you deserve it." They had kind of a "You made your bed, now lie in it" attitude.

Honestly, it's amazing that this man even had the guts to ask Jesus for help. What would make him take the chance of being rejected?

I believe he saw something in Jesus that distinguished him from the religious leaders. Yes, he was a great teacher and many believed him to be a prophet. Still, there was something in the way he interacted with people that made him seem more accessible. He seemed genuinely concerned about people. He saw them as souls, sons and daughters of God, and not subjects to be ruled over. Something in Jesus' demeanor convinced this man it was worth taking a chance on him and asking for help. I believe that deep inside, this leper knew Jesus would help. Otherwise, I don't think he'd have asked.

Jesus reached out his hand and touched the man. "I am willing," he said. "Be clean!" And immediately the leprosy left him (Luke 5:13).

He said "Yes!" Can you imagine the joy and excitement that must have overwhelmed this man when Jesus said, "I am willing, be clean"? His long, leprous nightmare was over! He was no longer among the walking dead, but he could come back to life, back to living among his family and his friends. It was as if he were being released from a prison of illness, and now he was free to live his life again. WHOOHOO!!

He was healed because of the willingness and the words that Jesus spoke.

Wait a minute: that sentence isn't actually correct.

It could have been. Jesus could have healed him with just a word, but he didn't. Instead, he went one step further. Notice the words, **"Jesus reached out his hand and touched the man."**

Do you see the significance?

Jesus touched the man with leprosy. According to Mosaic law, this made Jesus unclean. I'm sure anyone who was observing this interaction and the subsequent miracle gasped and as they saw Jesus reach out his hand. Knowing human nature, a few probably whispered, "Did you see Jesus touch him?" It was a bold, shocking move.

The *Zondervan NIV New Testament Commentary* says this about Jesus' actions:

In doing so, (touching the leper), Jesus demonstrated His decision to take our flesh upon Himself so that He might cleanse us from sin. His touching of the leper not only resulted in the leper being cured, but it also revealed Jesus' attitude toward the ceremonial law. He boldly placed love and compassion over ritual and regulation.[2]

I love that last line: "He boldly placed love and compassion over ritual and regulation."

That is what set Jesus apart from the religious leaders of his day. While they were all about maintaining the Law and making sure that every "t" was crossed and every "i" dotted, Jesus was doing the will of the Father.

The sad thing is that the religious leaders thought they were doing God's will. They were keeping the nation pure—avoiding another fall into compromise and sin. Yet they forgot the words of Micah 6:8 which say, **"He has shown you, O mortal, what is good. And what does the Lord require of you? To act justly and to love mercy and to walk humbly with your God."**

Jesus didn't forget. He knew the true, compassionate heart of God that says, **"Whoever comes to me I will never drive away" (John 6:37).**

When a leper, a ceremonially unclean man with a contagious disease, came asking for healing, Jesus didn't turn him away. He didn't run away and hide. He didn't throw stones, hoping to scare him off. Instead, he reached out his hand, touched him, and healed him.

Oddly enough, this incident reminds me of another time when the religious leaders would have liked Jesus to throw stones. The story is told in John 8:2–11.

At dawn he appeared again in the temple courts, where all the people gathered around him, and he sat down to teach them. The teachers of the law and the Pharisees brought in a woman caught in adultery. They made her stand before the group and said to Jesus, "Teacher, this woman was caught in the act of adultery. In the Law Moses commanded us to stone such women. Now what do you say?" They were using this question as a trap, in order to have a basis for accusing him.

But Jesus bent down and started to write on the ground with his finger. When they kept on questioning him, he straightened up and said to them, "Let any one of you who is without sin be the first to throw a stone at her." Again he stooped down and wrote on the ground.

At this, those who heard began to go away one at a time, the older ones first, until only Jesus was left, with the woman still standing there. Jesus straightened up and asked her, "Woman, where are they? Has no one condemned you?"

"No one, sir," she said.

"Then neither do I condemn you," Jesus declared. "Go now and leave your life of sin."

They were in the temple. The religious leaders knew the Law and they had skillfully planned a scheme to trap Jesus using it.

The woman caught in their plan meant nothing to them. She was just a pawn in their scheme—the bait used to set the trap. They honestly didn't care what happened to her—it was all about their power and their careers. Before they set the trap for Jesus, they trapped her.

She was petrified. Regrets raced through her mind like lightning.

"Why did I do it? How could I be so stupid to fall for him?"

Honestly, we don't know what happened. The Bible doesn't share the details of the affair with us. The only thing we do know is that she was a woman standing in the middle of a crowd waiting for her fate to be announced. She was a person with feelings and a soul, but the religious leaders didn't treat her like a person. They treated her like a tool to be used. In their self-righteous hypocrisy, they honestly didn't care if she lived or died.

Jesus did. He had seen the religious leaders try to trap him before, but this time they stooped to an all-time low. This time their trap didn't involve the hypothetical, but a human soul. Jesus saw the cold blackness of their hearts and knew they were just as guilty as the "sinner" they dragged before him. He cared what happened to her.

> *Jesus saw the cold blackness of their hearts and knew they were just as guilty as the "sinner" they dragged before him.*

Jesus knelt on the ground to write in the dirt. We will never know what Jesus wrote on the ground. (He didn't choose to humiliate them publicly the way they did her.) Still, they were persistent. They were demanding an answer from Jesus.

To throw stones or not to throw stones?

The answer he gave them was perfect. He shifted the burden of the decision to them when he said, **"Let any one of you who is without sin be the first to throw a stone at her."** One by one, they were forced to lay down their rocks and walk away. Instead of looking at what she had done, they had to look at what they did.

After her accusers dispersed, the woman was left alone with Jesus. He was the only one in the crowd who could have thrown a stone. He had no sin. Still, Jesus was not a stone thrower. He came to give life. That's what he offered this woman—a changed life.

Jesus didn't condemn her. Nor did he condone what she did. As they stood there, he did what was best for her eternal soul. He had saved her life from the religious leaders who wanted to kill her. Now he wanted to save her soul.

At this point you might be saying, "I'm not really seeing what these two scenarios have to do with each other. In one case, the man had a disease. In another, the woman was guilty of adultery. Where's the connection?"

I'm glad you asked!

The truth is it's difficult in our modern day society to relate to a leper. We no longer live in a world where a person with a disease is shunned by society or seen as evil because of a physical illness. Although doctors might still possibly quarantine an especially contagious patient, it would happen within a medical environment. Rather than the person with the illness being ignored, he would receive the best care possible from a team of medical professionals in an attempt to cure him and keep the disease from spreading.

If someone in a religious circle or church acquired an incurable, contagious disease, most Christians would feel compassion toward her. We would pray for her, and try to do whatever we could to encourage her in her time of need. Her family would be lovingly embraced and supported. I can't even imagine an instance where someone would be excluded or excommunicated from a church because of a physical ailment. We can be thankful that in our modern world, we are mostly past the days of seeing a suffering person and deeming them "Unclean!" because of a physical condition.

Unfortunately, we do not look always at those who are spiritually sick and dying through the same eyes. Too often in religious circles, we look at those who are like the woman caught in adultery as living obviously sinful lifestyles and we react like the religious leaders, crying, "Unclean!"

Rather than reaching out to these people with a message of hope and healing and offering them a new life in Jesus, we avoid them. We run away. We become stone throwers. While it sounds absolutely incredible that the rabbis in the New Testament would run away when a leper was approaching or throw rocks at the leper to keep him away, many religious people use their words as weapons to keep sinners away.

"I don't want them in my church."

"Those kids shouldn't be attending youth group with the church kids."

"She has no business coming to church dressed like that."

"Why should we do an outreach to that part of town?"

"She can't come back to this church—not after what she did."

Just like the religious leaders held to the letter of the Law because they were afraid of contamination, many religious people are doing everything they can to keep the church pure by keeping sinners out. This was never God's intention.

A few years ago, I heard an army Chaplain named Angel Berrios say, "We must engage our culture without entangling, contact without contaminating, and relate without compromising."

There are two sides to this quote. On the one hand, it is important that we do not compromise and become contaminated and entangled by the world. However, this is not done by shutting the world out. As we said in the last chapter, it was never God's will that Israel shut themselves off from those around them; it was his will that they be an *influence* on those around them.

As Christians, our job is to follow Christ and engage, contact, and relate to those in the world so they feel the love of Jesus and want to dedicate their lives to him. Our doors and our hearts should be open to everyone and anyone who is searching for God—no matter their race, age, gender, or even their sinful lifestyle. I'm not saying we should say the way they are living is right or condone their sin, but we should offer them a way out of their current situation and introduce them to the Savior who can forgive their sin and change their lives.

In the end, both the leper and the adulterous woman walked away from Jesus with the same thing: a new lease on life. After the leper presented himself to the priest, he was no longer labeled "unclean." He was allowed to go back to the temple, resume his normal life, and become an active part in the Jewish community again.

After the woman caught in adultery had her encounter with Jesus, she was no longer condemned. Jesus told her to go, leave her life of sin, and start a new life—no longer as a sinner, but as one of God's daughters.

In neither instance did Jesus follow in the footsteps of the religious leaders. He didn't see either case as too messy, too scandalous, too contaminating, or too "unclean" that his touch couldn't bring new life. No, with both the leper and the woman caught in adultery he applied mercy, compassion, and the heart of the heavenly Father who yearns for all men to come to the knowledge of truth and live holy lives.

Perhaps as you're reading these words, your heart is filling up with emotion. Maybe you've experienced the cruel, harsh treatment of "good Christian people" who didn't want you in their community. It's not unheard of. Unfortunately, it's all too common.

Recently, I heard the story of a Bible-believing church that went through a very difficult time because some of the people in the church disagreed with the leadership's decision to reach out to young people in their area. Apparently, part of the church didn't feel like it was appropriate for the church to be hosting events for "these types of teens."

We can be thankful that the leadership of the church did not bend to the pressure they were receiving. Rather than following in the footsteps of the rabbis and shutting the doors to the work of the Holy Spirit in the lives of these teens, they chose to follow in the footsteps of Jesus. They stood their ground and continued their outreach, even while some in the congregation gasped just as the onlookers did when Jesus reached out and touched the leper. They boldly placed love and compassion over ritual and regulation. Although some people left their church, their outreach continues to reach those who might otherwise never be touched with the message of the gospel.

That's the heart of Jesus—touching the untouchable, loving the unlovable, offering salvation to sinners rather than condemnation. Like he did for the leper, he is still changing lives. He's still offering new hope. He's still saying, "Come to me. Don't be afraid." **"Whoever comes to me I will never drive away" (John 6:37).**

If you come to him, like the leper, asking for spiritual healing and another chance at life, he will not turn you away.

He'll see beyond the labels, beyond your sin, beyond the reasons that others might say, "No, not you," and he will immediately forgive your sins and start you on the path to a new life. That's who he was, and that's who he is. After you experience his love, his forgiveness, and his spiritual healing, you will no longer be walking among the spiritually dead, but you will be alive and clean and ready to start your new journey with him.

Chapter 6 Questions

1. Has anyone ever thrown stones at you?

2. Can you remember a time when you responded by throwing stones rather than reaching out with compassion toward a hurting person?

3. One of the major differences between Jesus and the Jewish leaders was a sense of compassion. How can we place love and compassion over ritual and religion?

4. How can we practically "Engage our culture without entangling, contact without contaminating, and relate without compromising"?

5. How has Jesus' compassion changed your life?

Chapter 7

Demoniacs

It had come to this.
Alone.
Naked.
Uncontrollable.

ike a freak from a horror show, he lived among the tombs. At night, he roamed—sometimes in the mountains, other nights among the tombs—crying and cutting himself.

People were afraid of him. Parents held their children tightly anytime he was within viewing distance. This is what he had become. It had come to this.

He wasn't sure how he became this person. It was as if he was powerless in the face of the mighty evil that overtook his mind, body, and spirit. One day he was a normal man. Then he was "the demoniac," living among the tombs, naked and unkempt.

His life had become a nightmare. There were days when he wished he was in one of these tombs rather living among the dead. At least the dead had peace. This man had absolutely none.

[He was] a man with an unclean spirit, who had his dwelling among the tombs (Mark 5:2–3 KJV).

It appears from the biblical account that he'd been through a lot and this had been going on for a long time. Moving to the tombs seems to have been the last resort after everything else was tried.

This man lived in the tombs, and no one could bind him anymore, not even with a chain. For he had often been chained hand and foot, but he tore the chains apart and broke the irons on his feet. No one was strong enough to subdue him. Night and day among the tombs and in the hills he would cry out and cut himself with stones.

When he saw Jesus from a distance, he ran and fell on his knees in front of him (Mark 5:3–6).

Perhaps when the unclean spirit first came on him, his family and friends tried to help him. Maybe they thought "If we tie him up, we can keep him from hurting himself or anyone else. Maybe he will even be able to stay in his home and we'll take care of him."

But time after time, all of their efforts failed. Each time, when the unclean spirit was in control, he broke through the chains like a wild man. Once he was free, no one was safe. Who knew what he would do next? After many efforts to try to help him, control him, even tame him, they did what they had to do and they gave up on him. Just like him, they were powerless in the face of such uncontrollable evil.

The result was that he was left alone. **And always, night and day, he was in the mountains, and in the tombs, crying, and cutting himself with stones (Mark 5:5 KJV).**

What a horrible sight! He was a grown man wandering aimlessly, tortured and crying, driven by an evil spirit away from those he loved. All they could do was stand back and watch as he destroyed himself. Perhaps he wanted to kill himself as he cut himself with the stones—anything to make this horror end!

Still, it didn't end. Day after day, night after night, it continued. Unable to die, and yet completely unable to live, this man was a prisoner. Apparently, this went on for years. **For a long time this man had not worn clothes or lived in a house, but had lived in the tombs (Luke 8:27).**

The worst part is that it seemed there was no one who could set him free. Then Jesus appeared on the scene.

> **And [Jesus and the disciples] came over unto the other side of the sea, into the country of the Gadarenes. And when [Jesus] was come out of the ship, immediately there met him out of the tombs a man with an unclean spirit...But when he saw Jesus afar off, he ran and worshipped him (Mark 5:1–2 and 6 KJV).**

These verses make a very real point about those who are under the influence of demonic control: the human being and the spirit that controls them are not one and the same. They are separate and distinct.

On the one hand, you have the person under the control of the demonic influence—uncontrollable, frightening, running around naked, completely out of his mind.

On the other side of the coin, you have a human being. A prisoner that is being controlled by a demon. Notice it says he was crying. He didn't want to be controlled, he hated it, and he wept to be different. He didn't want his life to be this way—he just didn't know how to set himself free.

I believe that in these verses we see the human being making an attempt at freedom by throwing himself at the feet of Jesus. Even though the demons do most of the talking and do all they can to retain their control, somewhere inside of this man he mustered enough free will to put himself in Jesus' path to get help.

He shouted at the top of his voice, "What do you want with me, Jesus, Son of the Most High God? In God's name don't torture me!" (Mark 5:7).

Although it was the man speaking, the words came from the demon that was speaking through him. Notice how the demon admitted that he was in the presence of one who threatened his very existence.

For Jesus had said to him, "Come out of this man, you impure spirit!" (Mark 5:8).

At this point, the demon isn't thinking about the man it has controlled for so many years at all, because apparently Jesus told the demon to leave the man as soon as the man threw himself at Jesus' feet. Knowing that all power in heaven and earth was given to Jesus, the demon knew that its days inside of the man had come to an end. Now the demon is worried about its own future. It didn't want to be sent to the lake of fire to be tortured for the rest of eternity. Hence, it begs not to be tortured and starts negotiating.

Then Jesus asked him, "What is your name?"

"My name is Legion," he replied, "for we are many." And he begged Jesus again and again not to send them out of the area.

A large herd of pigs was feeding on the near-by hillside. The demons begged Jesus, "Send us among the pigs; allow us to go into them." He gave them permission, and the impure spirits came out and went into the pigs. The herd, about

two thousand in number, rushed down the steep bank into the lake and were drowned (Mark 5:9–13).

Jesus cast the demons out of the man, but he allowed them to go into the pigs. Have you ever wondered why? Of course, we'll never know for sure, but possibly it was to give clear evidence that the demons that were causing the man to be so destructive had left him and were now working their destruction through the pigs. We'll never really know the reasons for sure. What we do know is that neither the pigs nor the man who was formerly demon-possessed were ever the same.

Luke tells it this way, **"When those tending the pigs saw what had happened, they ran off and reported this in the town and countryside, and the people went out to see what had happened. When they came to Jesus, they found the man from whom the demons had gone out, sitting at Jesus' feet, dressed and in his right mind; and they were afraid. Those who had seen it told the people how the demon-possessed man had been cured" (Luke 8:34–36).**

You've got to stop and think about this picture.

The pig farmers probably weren't witnesses to the man's deliverance. Most likely, they were busy tending to their pigs. Then all of a sudden, the animals they were tending go berserk! The entire herd goes so crazy that it rushes down a steep hill and into a lake where they all drown!

If you're a pig farmer, you're asking yourself, "What just happened?"

So you go into the town and countryside, telling people about this absolutely bizarre, financially-devastating event. The people from the town hear about it and follow you back out of town to investigate what happened. When you all get there, you find Jesus and his disciples. What's more shocking is that the man that you know as the insane village demoniac is sitting at Jesus' feet, dressed and in his right mind.

Then those who witnessed the event tell you what happened.

Sadly, the people of the town didn't rejoice and throw a party for the man who had been delivered. Instead, they became afraid and angry about their financial losses. Rather than inviting Jesus to stay, they demanded that he leave immediately.

Then all the people of the region of the Gerasenes asked Jesus to leave them, because they were overcome with fear. So he got into the boat and left (Luke 8:37).

But what happened to the man who had been set free?

We'll have to return to the Gospel of Mark for that answer.

As Jesus was getting into the boat, the man who had been demon-possessed begged to go with him.

Jesus did not let him, but said, "Go home to your own people and tell them how much the Lord has done for you, and how he has had mercy on you."

So the man went away and began to tell in the Decapolis how much Jesus had done for him. And all the people were amazed (Mark 5:18–20).

In the morning, it appeared it would be just another day. To be honest, the townspeople would have preferred it that way. However, for the man possessed by a demon, that day was the best day of his life. It was the day that changed everything.

In the morning, he was a demoniac, condemned to live alone in the tombs. By nightfall, he was delivered, set free, in his right mind, and ready to become a disciple of Jesus.

Even though his only hope was actually dying when he woke up among the tombs that morning, by the end of the day his life was worth living. He had a purpose. He had a calling. There were so many people to tell what Jesus had done for him!

First, he went home to his family and told them all about the mercy God had shown him. Then, he went into the Decapolis (the league of ten heavily-populated Greek cities) and told them his story. When they heard his testimony, they responded in amazement. From a crazy, wild, uncontrollable demonic, to one of Jesus' first missionaries—all because he came into contact with the Great Deliverer—what an amazing story!

Even though his only hope was actually dying when he woke up among the tombs that morning, by the end of the day his life was worth living.

Throughout the Gospels, we see this story repeated over and over again—men and women who were controlled by demons were completely delivered and set free after an encounter with Jesus. In each of their stories, we can find hope. If they can go through deliverance and miraculously change so much, then we can, too.

Does that last phrase sound shocking to you? Are you asking yourself, "What is she talking about? I'm not living among the tombs, running around naked, and putting on demonic exhibitions like the demoniacs in the New Testament. How can he be an inspiration to me?"

Well, the simple truth is there is more to this world than the tangible things we can see, hear, touch, smell, and taste. These things belong to the physical world. However, beyond that world is the spiritual world. In the spirit world, there is a constant and ongoing battle between the forces of good and evil—God's kingdom and Satan's kingdom. Even though God has ultimately won the battle and Satan is ultimately defeated, the Prince of Evil is not content to be defeated alone. No, his mission is to destroy as many human lives as possible, keeping men and women under his control, hindering their relationship with God, and keeping them from living the abundant, victorious life God intends for us both on this earth and throughout eternity. Using every means at his disposal, Satan's goal is to control people, destroy them, and eventually cause them to spend eternity in hell with him. These are the orders he gives to demons each day: **"Steal and kill and destroy" (John 10:10).**

As we are living in the last days, demonic influences are rampant. We live in a culture that has rejected God and his ways as it chooses to embrace all forms of evil, including occultism, witchcraft, idol worship through false religions, and every kind of sexually deviant behavior imaginable. Psychics and mediums have hit television shows while movies tell stories of magicians, wizards, and curses controlling people's lives. These things are no longer on the fringes of our society, but are now pervasive in every area—including our playgrounds, our schools, our colleges, even our nurseries.

As our society has shifted to accept these things as normal, we've opened the door for a flood of demonic beings to influence, bind, and ultimately control people who either knowingly or unknowingly involved themselves in things that were far more dangerous than they ever expected. Like a hunter traps an animal, the enemy sets a trap using the bait of entertainment, peace through false religion, or unprohibited pleasure to lure his victims into sin and bondage from which they cannot escape.

Whether or not you want to believe it, we live in a culture where people are both demonically possessed and demonically oppressed. (People who are demon-possessed have completely rejected God and are allowing the demons to have full control of their lives. People who are demonically oppressed are not controlled by demons, however, they may still experience oppression from demonic forces they allow in their lives through dabbling in the occult, from tolerating sin in their lives, or from generational iniquities passed down from one generation to another.)

Personally, I have known people in both situations, and the sad truth is that in both cases, the individuals being influenced by the demons are not free to experience the abundant life Jesus died for them to live or to become the people God intended them to be. Just like the man who lived in the tombs, they are being robbed and destroyed by forces that seem to be beyond their control.

Yet, the good news is that the same Jesus who set captives free in the New Testament is still in the business of providing deliverance to captives today. There is hope! No matter what you've done or what's been done to you that has allowed the forces of evil to influence or control your life, it doesn't have to stay that way. There is still power in the name of Jesus and through his blood to break every chain that holds you captive.

Just like the man at the tombs, you can experience complete and total deliverance from any demonic influence that is controlling you or trying to influence you. Whether it's from dark thoughts controlling your mind, voices in your head, suicidal thoughts, uncontrollable addictions, or even explosive fits of anger, Jesus came to set you free.

Luke 4:18–19 says this about Jesus: **"The Spirit of the Lord is on me, because he has anointed me to proclaim good news to the poor. He has sent me to proclaim freedom for the prisoners and recovery of sight for the blind, to set the oppressed free, to proclaim the year of the Lord's favor."**

Today, the same hope available to the man at the tomb is available to you. The question is "Do you want to be free?"

You see, ultimately, the choice is up to you.

Deliverance is available to everyone who wants to be free; however, just like the man at the tombs had to cry out to Jesus for help, the first step in breaking the chains of demonic oppression that are controlling your life is voluntarily pursuing deliverance as an act of your free will.

Deliverance isn't magical—it doesn't just happen to you. You have to WANT to be free.

But, oh the freedom that is available to those who pursue it! Once you make up your mind that you don't want to live this way anymore—once you decide you don't want to be controlled by anything other than the power of the Holy Spirit—there is freedom and hope and joy greater than you could even imagine!

"The thief comes only to steal and kill and destroy; I have come that they may have life, and have it to the full" (John 10:10).

Just as he did in New Testament days, Jesus came to set captives free and take back all Satan has stolen from people. He wants to do this for any person who is experiencing demonic control or demonic oppression. He wants to deliver you and set you free so you can start experiencing the abundant life he has for you. Now the choice rests with you: Do you want to be free?

I'm sure at this point there are many who are saying, "Yes! How do I get started?"

Here's a few steps that our family has learned on our own pursuit to spiritual freedom:

1. **Start with prayer.** Get alone with God and tell him that you have decided of your own free will that you want to be free.

2. **Move on to repentance.** Confess any and all sin that you have been tolerating in your life—especially areas where you have dabbled in the occult, real or fantasy.

3. **Pray a prayer of spiritual deliverance** such as the one below:

Prayer of Confession and Deliverance[1]

Heavenly Father, I want to belong totally to you. I give you my body, soul, and spirit. I want you to reign supreme in every area of my life. I thank you, Lord Jesus, for dying on the cross for me. Please forgive me of every sin I have committed from birth until now. Put every sin underneath your blood. Forgive me for every sin _____ . (Name the sin and problem area such as anger, fear, unbelief, lust, etc.) Forgive me for every time I've been _____ . (Name the sin…angry, fearful, entertaining unclean thoughts or actions, using drugs, etc.)

Lord Jesus, forgive me if, through these sinful acts, I have given ground to any spirit that has Satan as master. I now take back all ground I have given to any spirit of Satan in _____ . (Name again the sin or problem areas, also any occult or other activities that you have been involved in.)

Forgive my parents, grandparents, and great grandparents of all their sins. If through their sins, they gave ground for any spirits of Satan to enter and control them, please forgive them. I take back all ground my forefathers may have given to Satan.

I command all spirits of Satan that are trying to attack me or oppress me to stop right now, to leave me right now and go into the pit forever, because I now belong to Jesus Christ who has conquered you wicked spirits, and your master, Satan. You have no legal right to me anymore.

I invite you, Holy Spirit, to come into my life and fill every part of my being with yourself. Give me the fruit of the Spirit, and give me those gifts of the Spirit you desire me to have. May your power, blessed Holy Spirit, flow through me, so that I may be a strong witness for the Lord Jesus Christ.

Thank you, Lord Jesus, for hearing my prayer.

4. In some cases, you may need to **seek the help of a pastor** experienced in deliverance ministry.

For my family, spiritual deliverance was a God-send. It completely changed our lives. When the oppression we were experiencing was removed, we were able to follow the Holy Spirit into each inner healing that he had for us. Today, we are completely different people because we went through the deliverance process and applied the biblical principles of the Word of God to our lives. Now, like the demoniac living in the tombs, we feel compelled by the Holy Spirit to share this part of our testimony and make other people aware of the incredible freedom that is still available today through the ministry of spiritual deliverance.

Just like the demoniac living in the tombs, no person has to live his or her life controlled by either unholy spirits or generational iniquities. Just as he did in the New Testament, Jesus sees beyond the effects of any demonic influence on your life, and sees YOU—a human being who needs to be set free. The same Jesus who provided freedom in the New Testament still offers that freedom today. The only question that remains is, do you want to be free?

Chapter 7 Questions

1. This chapter talks about separating the person from the demonic influences controlling the person. How can we follow Jesus' example in helping people?

2. How has the occult and participating in false religions become acceptable in American culture?

3. Are there any areas where you've allowed these things in your own life? What about through horoscopes? Ouija boards? Fantasy games? Psychics or mediums?

4. Do you think average Christians are more likely to tolerate witchcraft, magic, and false religions than

Chapter 8

Sinners

Have you ever wished you could be the life of the party? One of my secret wishes in life has always been that I would be the person everyone wanted to invite to their party—the fun person, the person who was at the top of the invite list. Sadly, this has never really been my lot in life. I'm a little too serious, and perhaps even a little too shy. Once I get to know you, we'll have lots of fun, but I'm not always comfortable letting my hair down among strangers.

I'm thankful that Jesus did not share my insecurities and inhibitions when he walked on the earth. Instead, he was the life of the party wherever he was invited. Reading though the New Testament, you can see he was invited to a lot of people's houses. For instance, in Luke 7:36–50, Jesus was invited to the home of Simon, the Pharisee. I don't know what Simon was expecting when he initiated the invitation, but it turned out to be a night that no one would forget!

When one of the Pharisees invited Jesus to have dinner with him, he went to the Pharisee's house and reclined at the table. A woman in that town who lived a sinful life learned that Jesus was eat-

ing at the Pharisee's house, so she came there with an alabaster jar of perfume. As she stood behind him at his feet weeping, she began to wet his feet with her tears. Then she wiped them with her hair, kissed them and poured perfume on them.

When the Pharisee who had invited him saw this, he said to himself, "If this man were a prophet, he would know who is touching him and what kind of woman she is—that she is a sinner."

Jesus answered him, "Simon, I have something to tell you."

"Tell me, teacher," he said.

"Two people owed money to a certain money-lender. One owed him five hundred denarii, and the other fifty. Neither of them had the money to pay him back, so he forgave the debts of both. Now which of them will love him more?"

Simon replied, "I suppose the one who had the bigger debt forgiven."

"You have judged correctly," Jesus said.

Then he turned toward the woman and said to Simon, "Do you see this woman? I came into your house. You did not give me any water for my feet, but she wet my feet with her tears and wiped them with her hair. You did not give me a kiss, but this woman, from the time I entered, has not stopped kissing my feet. You did not put oil on my head, but she has poured perfume on my feet. Therefore, I tell you, her many sins have been forgiven—as her great love has shown. But whoever has been forgiven little loves little."

Then Jesus said to her, "Your sins are forgiven."

The other guests began to say among them-selves, "Who is this who even forgives sins?"

Jesus said to the woman, "Your faith has saved you; go in peace."

Since Simon invited Jesus to his house, it was up to him to be hospitable toward Jesus. But this was not the case. He did not even do what was proper etiquette for a guest who entered his house at his invitation.

In that culture, it was the custom to greet the guest with a kiss. Simon did not.

It was proper to wash the guest's dirty feet. Simon did not.

It was the right thing to anoint the guest's head with oil. Simon did not. He invited Jesus, but that was the extent of his welcoming Jesus into his home or his life.

We see in Simon's actions and behavior that he is a very self-righteous man. He is arrogant, pompous, proud and full of himself. He was rude and condescending toward Jesus. He didn't believe Jesus was anything more than a man like himself. He may have even thought he was better than Jesus.

Jesus, on the other hand, tried to make himself at home in Simon's house. He reclined to eat, and he talked. He was kind, friendly, and honest. He was himself. Jesus knew he was being treated rudely, but he did what was proper on his part.

In comes the third person in our story—the town prosti-tute—entering Simon the Pharisees' house. Simon could not believe his eyes! He waited to see what Jesus would do since the woman went straight for Jesus.

Simon knew how he would handle it. He wanted to throw her out! How dare she have the audacity to enter his house? She was the town tramp! He knew how she lived. He knew all about her. He would never think of inviting someone like her! He would wait and see how Jesus handled the situation.

Exactly what gave her the courage to go to Simon's house, we'll never know. Obviously, she wanted to change her life. She probably heard all the talk about Jesus. Perhaps she watched him from afar for days or maybe even weeks. She watched how he responded to people, how he talked to them and treated them. After all, she wasn't going to take a chance and trust another man in her life. But as she watched him and listened to him speak, she wanted what he could offer her—a brand new life. She wanted to be born again. She wanted to live a different life. She wanted the pain in her heart to go away. She wanted more in life than to be used and abused by men. She wanted Jesus.

So into Simon's house she walked. She didn't care what anyone would think or say. She knew she was a sinner and wanted a brand new life.

But when she got to him, all she could do was cry. All the years of pain, insult, abandonment, and rejection came out in tears that fell on his feet. She poured the oil on his feet and cried and cried. She then used her hair to wipe his feet. Her heart was reaching out to him. She needed him.

Up to now, all she knew was pain in her life. He could help her. This day she was determined to get help. It had to be his help. He was her answer. She wanted change in her life. She wanted a brand new start. She needed his forgiveness and she got it.

Simon was indignant. He couldn't believe what his eyes were seeing! He couldn't believe Jesus was allowing such a woman to get near him, let alone touch him! This proved what Simon suspected all along—Jesus was nobody.

So Jesus was going to prove to Simon exactly who he was. To do so, he said, "Simon, let me show you what is inside your heart."

Then he proceeded to remind Simon that he did nothing to make him feel welcome. He did not even do what was expected of him. Jesus presented Simon with the fact that he, too, was a sinner just like this woman. Jesus knew Simon needed his forgiveness just as much as this woman. But Jesus also saw the biggest differences in their hearts. She was humble and repentant for her life and her sins. Simon had no humility, no repentant attitude, and thought too highly of himself.

Simon couldn't see he needed Jesus' forgiveness just like this woman. He justified his life and actions and behavior. He didn't live her life. He was married. He was decent. He wasn't like her. He had a good job, a respected job. He was a good person. People came to him for help. He didn't need this Jesus. He certainly didn't need to ask Jesus to forgive him. Forgive him for what?

The evening ended with two completely different people, Simon and the woman, choosing two very different paths in life. The woman was forgiven by Jesus. She believed that Jesus could forgive her sins and she lived the rest of her life for Jesus. He even praised her faith, blessed her to go live in peace.

The saddest commentary is that nowhere does it say Simon changed or repented for his sins, which in God's eyes are just as bad as the woman's. In fact, Simon's may be worse because he went on deceiving himself that he was so good, nothing was wrong with him and his life.

Think about it. He had Jesus right in his home, ate with him and never saw his personal need for a Savior. The fulfillment of every Jewish law and prophecy was standing right there in front of him, and this teacher of the law, this man of religion, couldn't wait for Jesus to go home. He just couldn't get over Jesus' willingness to associate with sinners.

As we continue to study the New Testament, we see that this was a constant source of contention between Jesus and the religious leaders. They simply could not understand his concept of forgiving and redeeming sinners. Instead, they preferred their ideas of condemnation and disassociation. For example, look how they reacted when Jesus chose a tax collector and sinner to be one of his disciples.

> **As Jesus went on from there, he saw a man named Matthew sitting at the tax collector's booth. "Follow me," he told him, and Matthew got up and followed him.**
>
> **While Jesus was having dinner at Matthew's house, many tax collectors and sinners came and ate with him and his disciples. When the Pharisees saw this, they asked his disciples, "Why does your teacher eat with tax collectors and sinners?"**
>
> **On hearing this, Jesus said, "It is not the healthy who need a doctor, but the sick. But go and learn what this means: 'I desire mercy, not sacrifice.' For I have not come to call the righteous, but sinners" (Matthew 9:9–13).**

"The healthy don't need a doctor, but the sick." With this one phrase, Jesus explained why he mingled with everyone and anyone who came seeking the kingdom of God.

Doctors come to heal sick people. They don't say, "Go make yourself better and then come see me." That would be ridiculous! A doctor's job is to heal. Jesus' job was to heal mankind's broken relationship to God. Why not start with the people who actually wanted to get better?

However, these words didn't simply explain Jesus' mission; they also told the Pharisees and other religious leaders they weren't doing their jobs right. They weren't even trying to help the people that needed the most help. Instead, they were avoiding them and making it virtually impossible for them to get help and restore their relationship with God. All the religious leaders wanted to do was congratulate themselves on how "spiritually healthy" they were. With this comment Jesus reminded them that the job of a spiritual leader is to be a doctor and lead sinners to repentance. That's what he was doing and it's what they should have been doing.

I love how he told them to **"Go and learn what this means: 'I desire mercy, not sacrifice.'"**

Can't you just picture their faces? "Did he just tell us to go learn something? Seriously?!"

This wasn't just any phrase—this was a direct quotation of Hosea 6:6, **"For I desire mercy, not sacrifice, and acknowledgement of God rather than burnt offerings."** He might as well have said, "Go school yourselves on the Old Testament." How dare he say this to men who considered themselves experts on Old Testament law and prophesy?

Perhaps it was because even though they considered themselves experts, they certainly weren't acting like they knew the meaning of Hosea 6:6. Otherwise, they wouldn't be consumed with following every jot and tittle of the Law and rabbinic tradition while they completely abandoned the concepts of benevolence or kindness toward others.

Funny, they didn't like what he had to say. They didn't take it to heart and say, "We need to change." Instead, they responded like Simon and hated him even more than they did before.

Ironically, even though the Jewish leaders hated Jesus, the tax collectors and sinners loved him. Why not? He was the only religious leader who offered them any hope. His message offered them forgiveness from sin, a new relationship with God, and a new life. He said, "God hasn't given up on you. He still wants you. If you will come to him, repent, and start following his ways, you can have a place in his kingdom."

Nowhere is this message expressed more beautifully than in Luke 15, where Jesus tells the parable of the lost coin, the parable of the lost sheep, and the parable of the prodigal son. However, it's very, very important that we look at Luke 15:1 and see to whom Jesus was speaking when he told this parable.

God loves sinners. He doesn't write them off as lost or hopeless, but he seeks them hoping they will repent and change their course and enter into a relationship with him.

Now the tax collectors and sinners were all gathering around to hear Jesus.

Sure, the Pharisees were there, too. But as usual, they were upset that Jesus was hanging out with sinners.

But the Pharisees and the teachers of the law muttered, "This man welcomes sinners and eats with them" (Luke 15:2).

It was in these circumstances, to these two groups of people, that Jesus spoke these three parables that have been repeated so often throughout history. They show the heart of the heavenly Father toward sinners.

God loves sinners. He doesn't write them off as lost or hopeless, but he seeks them, hoping they will repent and choose to change their course and enter into a relationship with him. Like the woman who lost the coin, he is passionate in his pursuit of sinners. Like the shepherd, he rejoices over each and every one that repents and returns to him. With a father's heart, he yearns for sinners to come to him. When they do, he runs to them, embraces them, and welcomes them back into his family.

Unlike the Pharisees who were quick to condemn and ostracize, the heavenly Father does not throw people away. His heart's desire is that all should come to repentance and restored fellowship with him. To this end, he constantly pursues sinners, offering them an invitation of both forgiveness and fellowship. As one last example, let's look at Luke 19:1–10 and the story of Zacchaeus.

Jesus entered Jericho and was passing through. A man was there by the name of Zacchaeus; he was a chief tax collector and was wealthy. He wanted to see who Jesus was, but because he was short he could not see over the crowd. So he ran ahead and climbed a sycamore-fig tree to see him, since Jesus was coming that way.

Zacchaeus worked for the Roman government as a tax collector. With that came a sense of power and authority. He used this power to exploit the people by overcharging them. If anyone came against him, he could tax them for everything they owned. As you can imagine, this did not make Zacchaeus very popular. He was definitely not at the top of the list to be invited to parties!

Then one day Jesus came to Zacchaeus' town. Zacchaeus wanted to see Jesus, but he was very short and knew it would be difficult to see over the other people. Certainly, no one was going to be doing him any favors and helping him see. So he climbed a sycamore tree. Who needs them?! From its branches, he could see the entire parade.

When Jesus reached the spot, he looked up and said to him, "Zacchaeus, come down immediately. I must stay at your house today."
So he came down at once and welcomed him gladly.

As Jesus walked by the sycamore tree, he stopped and looked up at Zacchaeus standing in the tree and said to him, "Come down here. I am coming home with you for dinner."

Zacchaeus must have been stunned! Jesus was surrounded by religious leaders, businessmen, healthy men, and good Jews. Yet Jesus didn't invite himself to their homes. He wanted to spend time with Zacchaeus.

I believe at that moment, Jesus had a friend and follower for life. In Jesus, Zacchaeus found love, acceptance, and friendship. Suddenly, he didn't feel alone. Someone wanted him. Someone saw his value as a person, not just his occupation. Instead of rejection and torment, Zacchaeus found love and acceptance. Even more, he found forgiveness. He no longer felt a need to prove anything to anyone except Jesus. Jesus wanted him.

All the people saw this and began to mutter, "He has gone to be the guest of a sinner."

Again, with the muttering!

But Zacchaeus stood up and said to the Lord, "Look, Lord! Here and now I give half of my pos-

sessions to the poor, and if I have cheated anybody out of anything, I will pay back four times the amount."

Jesus said to him, "Today salvation has come to this house, because this man, too, is a son of Abraham. For the Son of Man came to seek and to save the lost."

All the muttering in the world wouldn't deter Zacchaeus. Like the woman at Simon's party, and Matthew, and everyone who chooses to leave a life of sin, Zacchaeus was ready for a change. He wanted what Jesus had to offer—he was desperate for it. If Jesus really wanted him—if Jesus was really offering him forgiveness—then he was going to grab hold of it and never let go. To demonstrate his commitment, he made dramatic lifestyle changes. He was no longer going to live like a sinner, he was going to live like a follower of Christ.

Zacchaeus' life changed that day. He woke up a dirty, rotten tax collector. He went to bed a sinner saved by grace.

Why?

Because the Son of Man came to seek and to save the lost.

The story of Zacchaeus demonstrates the same truth as the other verses we've looked at in this chapter. To everyone, sinners and saints, tax collectors, prostitutes and Pharisees, Jesus comes and extends an invitation. He loves us and wants to change us. The decision is what we do with Jesus and what we allow Jesus to do inside of us.

> The fault never lies with Jesus. It is up to us and our free will if we accept Jesus or reject him.

The fault never lies with Jesus. It is up to us and our free will to either accept Jesus or reject him.

Throughout these chapters, we've seen two very distinct differences to Jesus' invitation. The woman, Matthew, and Zacchaeus were all born again. They wanted their lives changed. They knew they needed Jesus.

On the other hand, Simon and the other religious leaders were happy with themselves. They didn't want Jesus. They liked their lives the way they were. They had a title, prestige among the people, health, and money. They were satisfied.

The people they called "sinners" weren't satisfied. They wanted more. They needed more. They needed Jesus. The religious leaders didn't need Jesus. But the absolute truth is Jesus was available for both groups. It was up to them.

Today, the same choice stands before us that stood before the people in the New Testament. We all have free wills.

Are we going to be like the "sinners" who want Jesus to forgive them and received his forgiveness and a new life? Or are we going to be like Simon who was extremely pleased with himself and rejected Jesus?

That amazes me. If we want to stay the same, God allows it. Why would anyone want to stay the same? Why would anybody be so pleased with the way things are?

Life in Jesus Christ is available to whosoever wants it. Romans 3:23 says, **"For all have sinned and fall short of the glory of God."**

All of us are spiritually sick; all of us need the spiritual healing Jesus has to offer. Just like he did when he walked the earth, he still offers his salvation freely to anyone who will receive it. It is ours for the asking. There is no one that is too far gone for Jesus to save. When he looks at every human being, he says as he did to Zacchaeus, "He, too, is a child of God," and he invites you to come into fellowship with him.

The only question left is, Will you except his invitation?

Chapter 8 Questions

1. Who are you most like, the Pharisees or the sinners?

2. Do you see yourself as a sinner who needs Jesus Christ?

3. Do you want change in your heart and life?

4. Are you willing to allow Jesus to come in and do what he has to do inside of you?

5. Are you satisfied with yourself and feel you give God enough of yourself?

6. Do you struggle with self-righteousness?

7. Is that attitude keeping you from being honest with yourself and making the necessary changes in your life?

Chapter 9

Jesus and Children

*D*id you ever meet a man who really enjoyed being around children?

Even as I write that question, I think of a dear friend of our family. Whenever a mom brings a child into his office, his face brightens and he stops and talks directly to the child. Better yet, he stops and listens as his little friend tells a story about stuffed animals or what happened at home. For those brief moments, he treats that child as though whatever he or she is saying is the most important thing in the world.

He isn't just like this with his patient's kids. I remember watching him with his own children as they were growing up. He loved being a dad! Over the years I've heard him tell stories of taking his daughters to breakfast and listening to all the details about who likes whom and who isn't talking to whom in elementary school. I've never seen a father more disappointed when his sons went off to college and there were no more sporting events and practices to attend. Now that his kids are grown and married, I know he's eagerly awaiting grandchildren and a new generation of kids. That's just the way he is—he sees the value in children.

My brother, Jamie, is another guy who sees the value in kids, and they, in turn, love hanging out with him! I remember when he decided that we were going to coach the Junior Bible Quiz team at our church. To be honest, when I first heard about it, I was a little skeptical. It seemed a little hokey to me. Jamie, on the other hand, knew right away that the Holy Spirit was calling him to this position. He saw it as "young men's ministry"—coaching his team of four little boys and one girl.

Over the course of that JBQ season, he taught them not only facts about the Bible and Bible verses, but how to stand when a woman walks into the room and to hold doors for a lady (including the little girl in class). Rather than sticking to a strict schedule, he listened to their stories and answered their questions. In fact, he was such an awesome coach that the next year he had two teams because so many kids wanted to join. Even though he'd always complain about how early he had to get up to get to JBQ practice every week, I knew that when practice was over, I'd hear, "They were so funny this week. Wasn't that cute? I'm so glad we went, that was so much fun."

It's a beautiful thing when a man sees value and significance in children. In fact, it's a very Christlike quality. As we'll see in this chapter, when Jesus walked on earth, he saw children as significant in God's kingdom. We know because in between teaching, healing, casting out demons, and dealing with the ridiculousness of the Pharisees, Jesus took time and paid special attention to children. When others tried to push the children aside as insignificant and unimportant, Jesus said, "Don't you dare."

Let's read about it:

**People were also bringing babies to Jesus for him to place his hands on them. When the disciples saw this, they rebuked them. But Jesus called the children to him and said, "Let the little children come to me, and do not hinder them, for the kingdom of God belongs to such as these. Truly I tell you, anyone who will not receive the king- dom of God like a little child will never enter it"
(Luke 18:15–17).**

The storyline is simple. Jesus was teaching among a group of people, most likely a crowd. People, probably mothers and fathers, sister and brothers, maybe even a few grandmas and grandpas, started bringing their children to Jesus to have him bless them. In Jewish culture, it was quite normal for people to bring small children to great men to have them blessed. If you're going to take your little ones to someone to be blessed, who would be greater than Jesus?

For some reason, the disciples became annoyed at all the children gathering round. They saw them as bothersome and unimportant—insignificant. How could these people expect Jesus to take a break from all of the important things he was doing to pay attention to a bunch of rug rats?

However, when Jesus saw what was going on, he realized he should have been paying more attention to the disciples. What were they doing, turning the children away?

Can't you just picture Jesus saying, "Guys, what are you doing? I don't want you to send them away; I want you to bring them here!"

Then, he pointed out that the disciples could learn a thing or two from the children they were turning away. He says, **"Anyone who will not receive the kingdom of God like a little child will never enter it."**

What does that mean?

John MacArthur says "This verse pictures faith as the simple, helpless, dependence of those who have no resources of their own. Like children, they have no achievements and no accomplishment to offer or with which to commend themselves."[1]

I guess he was saying, "Hey guys, you're turning away children because you think what we're doing here is too important to be bothered with them.

Get over yourselves. These kids—they are the future of the kingdom of God. Unless you stop looking for power, prestige, and popularity and start following me in humility and faith, you're not going to enter the kingdom of heaven. There's no room for that stuff in my kingdom. In my kingdom, a leader is a servant to all—even little children."

In that public rebuke of the disciples Jesus accomplished two things. First, he corrected the disciples' course and taught them what their attitude needed to be as his followers. Perhaps more importantly, he showed the entire world the heavenly Father's heart toward children. In God's kingdom, they are important. They are significant. Most importantly, they are welcome.

And he took the children in his arms, placed his hands on them and blessed them (Mark 10:16).

When I was a kid growing up in Sunday School, there were always pictures attached to felt storyboards to go with this story. The pictures portrayed a rather wimpy, pious-looking Jesus reaching out his hand and solemnly "blessing the children." However, the more I read and study the Bible, I get a different picture in my mind.

Instead, I see a really robust, muscular, good-looking guy reaching down and lifting the children onto his lap. Remember, Jesus was a carpenter—he was no wimp. He was probably pretty buff from years of hard work. Also, as the oldest brother in a large family, Jesus was used to being around kids—first his brothers and sisters and then nieces and nephews.

I picture him with a big smile on his face, talking and laughing with the kids. I'd imagine his eyes were sparkling as he listened to their stories about the trip here and everything that happened along the way. Maybe he even comforted a few who were afraid of strangers.

When he did lay his hands on them and pray, I'm sure he used words that the kids could understand. I can picture him waving as the kids walked away, and chuckling as a child did something especially adorable. As the kids got back to their parents, I'm sure they told stories of everything the "nice man" said to them and how he prayed.

It was an event they'd never forget. I'm sure he left an impression on the minds of the parents, too. Don't parents always remember the people who are especially kind to their kids? Here was a teacher that not only took time to bless their kids, but he did it in such a personal way. Even when his followers tried to push them aside, he didn't. He said, "Come."

Jesus was different. Jesus saw everyone—even children—as significant.

Although certainly the most popular, it is not the only time that Jesus made his views about the significance of children known. Ironically enough, it was when Jesus was once again correcting the disciples' wrong ideas about greatness. (They really struggled with the concept of servanthood.)

At that time the disciples came to Jesus and asked, "Who, then, is the greatest in the kingdom of heaven?"

He called a little child to him, and placed the child among them. And he said: "Truly I tell you,

unless you change and become like little children, you will never enter the kingdom of heaven. Therefore, whoever takes the lowly position of this child is the greatest in the kingdom of heaven. And whoever welcomes one such child in my name welcomes me" (Matthew 18:1–5).

Can't you just picture Jesus rolling his eyes and sighing, "Here we go again. When are these guys going to stop competing for greatness?" Of course, he knows when it will end. He knows what's coming—not an earthly kingdom, but a cross. They'll learn, but for now he'll try one more time to explain it.

Noticing a child in the crowd, he smiles and says, "Come over here, I've got a job for you." Anyone who's ever given a child an important job knows how pleased they are to serve.

Taking the child on his lap he says, "Guys, listen, **unless you change and become like little children, you will never enter the kingdom of heaven. Therefore, whoever takes the lowly position of this child is the greatest in the kingdom of heaven. And whoever welcomes one such child in my name welcomes me."**

It's interesting. When the disciples are trying to figure out who's the greatest in their group, Jesus says, "Imitate the lowly position of this child."

Then Jesus continues,

"If anyone causes one of these little ones—those who believe in me—to stumble, it would be better for them to have a large millstone hung around their neck and to be drowned in the depths of the sea" (Matthew 18:6).

All of the commentaries are quick to point out that "little ones" doesn't refer to literal children, but to those who are like children. Still, I can't help but wonder if the same standard wouldn't apply to literal children. Seeing how much love Jesus had for children, how would he feel about those who treat children badly, placed things in their lives that cause them to stumble spiritually, and established barriers in their lives that keep them from entering the kingdom of God? It seems reasonable to me that if he felt so strongly about those who damaged those who were like children, he would be equally appalled at those who damaged the souls of real children.

Of course Jesus didn't just *teach* about children being valuable. Several times throughout his ministry, we see him changing his plans and stopping to minister to the needs of a child.

Luke 9 tells the story of Jesus healing a child who was possessed by a demon.

John 4 tells of Jesus healing the son of a Roman official.

In Mark 5, we have the touching story of Jesus raising a little girl from the dead.

Who can forget the little boy who supplied the lunch that Jesus multiplied to feed over five thousand people?

Sometime after this, Jesus crossed to the far shore of the Sea of Galilee (that is, the Sea of Tiberias), and a great crowd of people followed him because they saw the signs he had performed by healing the sick. Then Jesus went up on a mountainside and sat down with his disciples. The Jewish Passover Festival was near.

When Jesus looked up and saw a great crowd coming toward him, he said to Philip, "Where shall we buy bread for these people to eat?" He asked this only to test him, for he already had in mind what he was going to do.

> **Philip answered him, "It would take more than half a year's wages to buy enough bread for each one to have a bite!"**
>
> **Another of his disciples, Andrew, Simon Peter's brother, spoke up, "Here is a boy with five small barley loaves and two small fish, but how far will they go among so many?" (John 6:1–9).**

If you read the other Gospel accounts about this miraculous meal, there is no mention of where they got the loaves and the fish. However, the Gospel of John adds this very significant detail: **the food came from a little boy.**

A few years ago, I had the privilege of teaching a class of three- to five-year-olds during the Wednesday night service at our church. One thing I learned quickly is that they loved to be helpers. No matter how small the task—passing out plates at snack time or even helping clean up, they beamed with pride that they were chosen to be an assistant.

As I read the story of Jesus feeding the five thousand, I can almost imagine the face of the child as he is chosen out of the crowd to be the catalyst for this miraculous event. I'm sure he went home and told everyone who would listen how the teacher called him over and asked if he'd be willing to share his lunch. After Jesus prayed, it was his little lunch that was multiplied to feed over five thousand people—and there were leftovers! Certainly, this was a day that the boy would never forget!

> **Jesus said, "Have the people sit down." There was plenty of grass in that place, and they sat down (about five thousand men were there). Jesus then took the loaves, gave thanks, and distributed to those who were seated as much as they wanted. He did the same with the fish.**

When they had all had enough to eat, he said to his disciples, "Gather the pieces that are left over. Let nothing be wasted." So they gathered them and filled twelve baskets with the pieces of the five barley loaves left over by those who had eaten (John 6:10–13).

I wonder if the boy stuck around to count how many baskets of food were left? I'd imagine he felt pretty important hanging out with Jesus and the disciples, watching them pass his lunch around and then collect the leftovers. Knowing the kind of man he was, I'm sure Jesus made sure to thank the little guy for being willing to share and be a part of what he was doing. This had to be one of the best days of this boy's life—all because Jesus allowed him to play a significant role in a magnificent event.

You might be thinking, "Don't you think you're stretching this a little far? Maybe this kid was the only one who had a lunch available and it was all coincidence."

I don't think so. The fact is Jesus didn't need any food to do this miracle. If he could make this tiny lunch feed so many people, then he could have just as easily turned rocks or dirt into food. For that matter, he could have brought his own lunch and shared that with the people! But instead, he chose to include an insignificant child with a meager lunch in his plan. He allowed a child, who most people probably didn't even notice in the crowd, to be included forever in the biblical account of the Gospel story.

Not only are children welcome in God's kingdom, but God intends that they play a significant role.

Perhaps he did it to make a statement—to remind all people throughout time that children are very welcome in the kingdom of God. Not only are they welcome, but God intends that they play a significant role. Just as he did when he walked the earth, Jesus is still saying, **"Let the little children come to me, and do not hinder them, for the kingdom of God belongs to such as these."**

Chapter 9 Questions

1. How was Jesus' attitude toward children different than the disciples'?

2. Is your attitude more like Jesus' or the disciples'?

3. If every Christian in today's church adopted Jesus' attitude toward children, how would our churches be different? How would our world be different?

4. How can we help the children in our lives see themselves through Jesus' eyes?

5. What does the disciples' struggle with a desire for greatness tell us about their own battle with insignificance?

6. In your own struggle for significance, do you ever find yourself trying to prove your worth through accomplishments, success, or a prominent position?

Chapter 10

Women

Several years ago, *A Wellrounded Woman Magazine* ran a series about Jesus' interactions with women as he walked on the earth. With each new edition I was more and more convinced that Jesus was very different from most of the men I'd ever encountered.

You see, I grew up in an area where men tend to be very demeaning toward women. Have you ever seen a TV show where men sat around and had women waiting on them hand and foot? Or even worse, did you ever watch a show where the men sit in one room to eat at a party while women all sit in the kitchen, separate from the men? Welcome to my early childhood!

This is how the men acted at the church where I grew up. They saw themselves as superior to women, and they used Scriptures like "Wives, submit to your husband" as a mandate to make their wives into personal servants. In our area, abuse of all forms was common—not talked about—but common. Women, for the most part, were treated like second-class citizens.

Personally, I grew up with a father like this. My dad was an insecure man who chose not to deal with the issues in his soul. Throughout my life our relationship has been dominated by his insecurity.

When I was in second grade I transferred from public school to Christian school. I loved the environment and thrived on the curriculum. I quickly excelled. Instead of being proud and encouraging me to keep up the good work, his insecurities arose. He became hypercritical of everything I did. It was like he always had to point out that he was smarter by criticizing me.

When I became a teenager, he always told me I wanted too much out of life. He told me my standards were too high. Instead of supporting my dreams, he wanted to keep me in reality.

When I went to college and became class president, he hated it. I had stepped over the line of what a woman should do. I couldn't do anything to please him. My personality was too strong. I talked too much and too loudly.

My dad's attitude toward me left me with a lot of confused ideas. Is this how God felt about women? Did God really want women to squelch their personalities and capabilities to make men feel better? Did all men feel the way my dad did?

By the time I graduated from college these questions were tying me up in knots. To a point, I had lost myself, trying to be the kind of woman a man would want. The original me was all locked up in a box, while I was trying to be someone I wasn't. I wasn't happy and God wasn't pleased.

That's when God opened my eyes to see that my dad was wrong. The problem wasn't my outspoken personality or my high dreams and goals—the problem was my dad's insecurities. It took a while to work through the lies and the pain of my dad's rejection, but I am so happy that God set me free to be who he created me to be.

Today I know the answers to my questions. God does not share my dad's attitude toward women. In fact, God has the exact opposite feelings about women. God loves women. He created each one of us with a unique personality and individual capabilities and gifts. He wants to develop what he placed in us to the fullest potential. In fact, I have learned over the years that rather than crushing my growth, God is pushing me to grow. He thinks I am stronger, more capable, and able to do more things than I ever thought I would do.

Contrary to my earthly father, my heavenly Father has expanded my abilities in areas I never dreamed or even wanted to learn about. He is constantly stretching my knowledge and skills. He doesn't say, "You shouldn't try that." Instead, he says, "Let's try something new." It is my job to follow God in the paths that he chooses.

The Bible says in Galatians 3:28, **"There is neither Jew nor Gentile, neither slave nor free, nor is there male and female, for you are all one in Christ Jesus."** As we will see in this chapter, this is the way that Jesus treated all the women he came in contact with when he walked the earth. In his eyes, they were equal to men, and they had a place in his kingdom. One of the best examples of this is found in a few little verses tucked away in Luke 8:1–3.

> **After this, Jesus traveled about from one town and village to another, proclaiming the good news of the kingdom of God. The Twelve were with him, and also some women who had been cured of evil spirits and diseases: Mary (called Magdalene) from whom seven demons had come**

out; Joanna the wife of Chuza, the manager of Herod's household; Susanna; and many others. These women were helping to support them out of their own means."

I love these verses!

Joanna was the wife of Chuza, the manager of Herod's household. She had social rank, influence, and great wealth. Most importantly, she believed in Jesus with her whole heart. She loved him and wanted to help his ministry in every way she could.

She recognized that Jesus and his disciples had financial needs while they traveled around ministering. So she and other women like her decided to provide for those financial needs. The best part is Jesus accepted their offer. He allowed them to serve God in the capacities they had.

He didn't become insecure about taking help from women.

He didn't point out that finances weren't really a women's issue.

He didn't let his ego inflate and remind them that he miraculously got money out a fish when he needed to pay his taxes. He didn't really need their help. Jesus knew who he was, so he allowed them to be themselves and minister to him. Isn't he awesome?

Another example of Jesus' interactions with women comes from his friendship with Mary and Martha. These two women and their brother, Lazarus, shared a unique position in the New Testament: they were friends with Jesus. Actually, that sentence says a lot about them.

Friends were a rarity to Jesus. He was constantly surrounded by people who needed something from him. The religious leaders hated him and listened to every word he said to entrap him. When they invited him to a dinner, he was under scrutiny.

It wasn't this way at a friend's house. Their home was a refuge for him—a place where he could go and relax in the company of people who loved him and wanted to give something to him.

> **As Jesus and his disciples were on their way, he came to a village where a woman named Martha opened her home to him. She had a sister called Mary, who sat at the Lord's feet listening to what he said.**
>
> **But Martha was distracted by all the preparations that had to be made. She came to him and asked, "Lord, don't you care that my sister has left me to do the work by myself? Tell her to help me!"**
>
> **"Martha, Martha," the Lord answered, "You are worried and upset about many things, but few things are needed—or indeed only one. Mary has chosen what is better, and it will not be taken away from her" (Luke 10:38–42).**

Again, this is one of my favorite passages in the Bible. There are so many interesting nuances in this story that I've written and taught about it over and over again—usually focusing on our need to overcome our "Martha" tendencies and focus on what's important like Mary did. However, as I was writing this chapter, the Holy Spirit showed me something new. For the first time, he showed me that this Scripture is a

It was a revolutionary moment when Jesus said women were welcome to be part of his kingdom.

landmark invitation for women to participate in the kingdom of God.

Think about it: According to all common standards, Martha was doing the right thing. As the woman of the house, she was fulfilling her duty as hostess and making sure that everything was just right for her guest. Both socially and culturally, it was expected that the women would be busy preparing the meal and showing the warm hospitality customary in Jewish households.

Mary was the one who was going against the tide by sitting at Jesus' feet and listening to him speak. After all, Lazarus was there to entertain the guest. Mary should have been helping Martha prepare the meal.

However, when the issue was brought to his attention, Jesus didn't tell Mary to get back in the kitchen. Instead, he invited Martha to come and join Mary in choosing what was best—spending time with Jesus, learning from him, and being a part of what he was doing.

I wonder how many people were shocked at Jesus' words? He didn't chastise Mary? He invited Martha to join them?

It was a revolutionary moment—a liberating moment. A new precedent was being established as he said, "Men and women are both welcome to sit at my feet and learn from me and be a part of my kingdom."

Jesus' relationship with Mary and Martha doesn't end with this event. We see him interacting with them again in John 11. However, this time he wasn't coming for a friendly visit. He was arriving on the scene of a tragedy—they were upset that he was three days late.

Now a man named Lazarus was sick. He was from Bethany, the village of Mary and her sister Martha. (This Mary, whose brother Lazarus now

lay sick, was the same one who poured perfume on the Lord and wiped his feet with her hair.) So the sisters sent word to Jesus, "Lord, the one You love is sick" (John 11:1–3).

So when he heard that Lazarus was sick, he stayed where he was two more days, and then he said to his disciples, "Let us go back to Judea" (John 11:6–7).

So then he told them plainly, "Lazarus is dead" (John 11:14).

Lazarus became gravely ill. They sent word to Jesus, telling him of the sickness and begging him to come and help. However, Jesus didn't go right away. During his delayed return, Lazarus died, leaving Mary and Martha alone in a male-dominated world. Jesus had his reasons for not going right away, but Mary and Martha didn't know this. All they knew was Lazarus was dead, and Jesus hadn't come to help.

When Jesus arrived, he was instantly greeted by Martha. In extreme emotional pain and grief, she said to Jesus, "Lazarus could have lived if you had been here!" Jesus was greeted by the same sentiment from Mary. They were filled with disappointment—not unbelief—disappointment. They were shocked at what happened. They were confused. They were grieving.

How did Jesus respond to these two hurting women? John 11:33–35 tell us,

When Jesus saw her weeping, and the Jews who had come along with her also weeping, he was deeply moved in spirit and troubled. "Where have you laid him?" he asked.

"Come and see, Lord," they replied.

Jesus wept.

He didn't lash out at them. He didn't give them a lecture. He didn't say, "Who are you to talk to me like that?" He didn't silence or suppress their emotions. Instead, the Bible says Jesus was stirred to tears. He allowed himself to be touched by these women's emotional outbursts. He understood their pain. He listened to their hearts. He heard the words they spoke and responded in a loving, helpful manner.

Jesus was moved by their heartache. He identified with their pain. He didn't say, "Come on, ladies, get a grip. This is what God wanted." No, he cried with them. He comforted them. He was moved by their agony. He hurt because he saw the emotional pain these women were suffering.

Jesus wasn't offended by their questions. He didn't call their words a sin. He understood they were shocked and disappointed. Even though he knew this was all a part of God's plan, he understood that they didn't know God's plan. He didn't criticize or judge them.

He wasn't harsh with them. Rather, he cried because he understood how difficult it was for these women to live through the plans God had orchestrated. His heart went out to them. His love for Mary and Martha caused him to weep with them.

Then he raised Lazarus from the dead.

The more we study Jesus' interactions with women, the more we understand the heart of God toward women. As we understand our heavenly Father's heart, we will begin to see ourselves in new eyes.

In the eyes of God, women are special. We are significant. Although he sees us as being equal in value to men and equally welcome and usable in his kingdom, he also appreciates our uniqueness. Because he created us, he knows the unique challenges we face. Rather than running from the differences, he embraces them. He delights in them. When these differences create pain in our hearts, our minds, and our bodies, he doesn't run away. Instead, he is there to help us, just as he did when he walked the earth.

Nowhere is this fact better exemplified than in the story of Jesus' encounter with a woman in Mark 5:21–34.

> When Jesus had again crossed over by boat to the other side of the lake, a large crowd gathered around him while he was by the lake. Then one of the synagogue leaders, named Jairus, came, and when he saw Jesus, he fell at his feet.
>
> He pleaded earnestly with him, "My little daughter is dying. Please come and put your hands on her so that she will be healed and live." So Jesus went with him.
>
> A large crowd followed and pressed around him. And a woman was there who had been subject to bleeding for twelve years. She had suffered a great deal under the care of many doctors and had spent all she had, yet instead of getting better she grew worse.
>
> When she heard about Jesus, she came up behind him in the crowd and touched his cloak, because she thought, "If I just touch his clothes, I will be healed."
>
> Immediately, her bleeding stopped, and she felt in her body that she was freed from her suffering.
>
> At once Jesus realized that power had gone out from him. He turned around in the crowd and asked, "Who touched my clothes?"
>
> "You see the people crowding against you," his disciples answered, "and yet you can ask, 'Who touched me?' "

But Jesus kept looking around to see who had done it. Then the woman, knowing what had happened to her, came and fell at his feet and, trembling with fear, told him the whole truth.

He said to her, "Daughter, your faith has healed you. Go in peace and be freed from your suffering."

It had been a long time since she had felt really well. The disease in her body dominated her days and consumed her mind. She tried to function as well as she could, but ultimately, her sickness limited her.

The constant loss of blood left her body weak and exhausted. Living with hormones that never balanced themselves affected her mind and emotions. Because Jewish culture deemed women who were menstruating "unclean," she had to live with that stigma. Her illness was interfering with her marriage, her family, her friendships, and her ability to worship God at the temple. She was desperate to be free.

Over the past twelve years she had tried everything. She went from doctor to doctor, trying all their cures. They took her money, but nothing helped. She felt so alone. The doctors had no more answers. Most of the people in her life who started off supporting her lost interest. She needed help desperately—God was her only hope.

Then Jesus arrived in her town. Everyone in Israel had heard about him. The stories of the miracles he performed were remarkable and she needed Jesus to change *her* life with a miracle. That hope is what drove her out into the crowds that day–the deep desire for a miracle from Jesus.

Everywhere Jesus went he was surrounded by crowds of people wanting to hear him speak or experience a miracle. Just as she was making her way toward the crowd, a very important man interrupted. His name was Jarius. He was a ruler in the Jewish synagogue. He came to Jesus with a life-and-death emergency. His little girl was dying. The entire crowd turned to follow Jesus and Jarius and see what would happen. Would the little girl live or die?

As the crowd hurried toward Jarius' home, this woman couldn't believe what was happening. She needed help, too. She desperately wanted Jesus to heal her. She had nowhere else to turn.

That's when she made the decision to touch Jesus. She thought, "Maybe if I can just touch him I will be healed. I don't need his personal attention. The whole crowd doesn't have to be interrupted. Maybe if I just touch him, I can be free from my suffering."

So she weaved her way through the crowd to get as close to Jesus as possible. Then she reached out and touched the edge of his garment. Immediately, she knew she was healed. For the first time in years, she felt good—really good. She was just about to breathe a sigh of relief when the crowd stopped.

Jesus stopped the crowd and asked, "Who touched me?"

She was afraid. Would he be angry that she touched him? Would he embarrass her? Could she lose her miracle? With all these questions racing through her mind, she gathered all of her courage and stepped forward.

As soon as she saw his eyes, she knew she had nothing to fear. They were filled with kindness, compas-

Jesus wants each of us to know that women and their unique physical experiences are important to him.

sion, and understanding. He didn't stop the crowd to embarrass her. He stopped to acknowledge her.

You see, Jesus knew who touched him even before he asked. He knew all about her. He knew she had suffered for years. He knew she was desperate for help and today, he helped her.

Jesus treated this woman's problem like a sickness. He healed her. Most of the people in the crowd were concerned about the life-and-death crisis of a prominent ruler. To them, nothing could be more important. To Jesus, this woman and her "feminine problem" were important.

I believe he wants each of us to know that women and their unique physical experiences are important to him. He wants to help each of us. Jesus understands women and their bodies—from PMS to pregnancy and menopause. He understands because he created us. He knows how our bodies work. He knows women experience real physical symptoms that can cause real pain and suffering.

Look at how he treated this woman. He spoke tenderly to her and called her "Daughter." He showed her compassion, concern, and understanding. He stopped everything just to help her.

He wants to be there for us in the same way. Jesus wants to help each of us as we go through our own personal feminine issues. To him, women are important and what we go through is important. He wants to show us the same compassion, concern, and understanding he showed her.

We see in this passage, as well as all the passages we've studied, that Jesus is a tremendous supporter of women. Whether he's opening doors and breaking down barriers, inviting us to have a place in his kingdom or helping us through the hard times, he is a strong tower we can rely on. Rather than running from our emotions or trying to squelch them, he listens and really hears our hearts. Then he ministers to our need, whether it is physical, emotional, or spiritual.

The fact is that Jesus loves women, with a pure, holy love. He's not trying to make us into men or suppress us as slaves. Instead, his goal for women is the same as it is for men: to mold us and shape us into the image of himself so we can fulfill our purpose in his kingdom. What an awesome God we serve!

Chapter 10 Questions

1. Have you ever been treated badly by a man?

2. What effect did this have on your image of God and your relationship with him?

3. It was a revolutionary idea that Jesus allowed women to play a role in his ministry. What do the examples of Joanna and the other women, Mary and Martha, speak to you about your own role in God's kingdom?

4. What does looking at Jesus' compassionate response to Mary and Martha tell you about your own relationship with Jesus?

5. As we studied Jesus' heart toward women, what stood out most to you? Why?

Chapter 11

Widows

*B*efore we leave our study of Jesus and women too quickly, I'd like to look at a special group of women to whom Jesus gave special attention. As we study the New Testament, it seems that Jesus had a very soft spot in his heart for widows. It's not hard to understand why.

Being a widow in New Testament times wasn't easy. In fact, widowhood in that society was very difficult. Unless a widow had a son or a son-in-law who would take her into his house and care for her, she was destined to a life of extreme poverty. Even if a widow's financial needs were provided for, she still struggled with loneliness, grief, and a myriad of other emotions that made life hard.

As Mary's son, Jesus saw the life of a widow up close and personal. Perhaps that's why his heart was so tender toward them, and he helped them whenever he could. I wonder if his thoughts turned toward his own mom as he entered the town of Nain. I'm sure he was thinking about the important role a son played in the life of a widow when he performed one of his most outstanding miracles for a widow who was in the process of burying her son.

Soon afterward, Jesus went to a town called Nain, and his disciples and a large crowd went along with him. As he approached the town gate, a dead person was being carried out—the only son of his mother, and she was a widow. And a large crowd from the town was with her (Luke 7:11–12).

The funeral procession was moving down the street of the Galilean city of Nain. Honoring the dead was an important Jewish tradition. The body was usually wrapped and carried on a type of stretcher while the relatives followed behind the body.

Can you imagine what this woman was feeling?

Today it was her son being buried. She had made this walk before, burying her husband. Now as a widow she walked alone to bury her only beloved son.

She felt like her heart was going to break into a thousand pieces. Her head was hanging low. She couldn't swallow because of the lump in her throat. She had so many emotions as she walked down the street.

She was also scared. What would happen to her now? Where would she end up? She had seen this happen to other widows whose sons died. Their financial means were gone and they became penniless with no other option than to beg for food.

Scared, frightened, alone, and brokenhearted, she moved closer to the burial place. Just then she looked up.

When the Lord saw her, his heart went out to her and he said, "Don't cry" (Luke 7:13).

Her eyes, filled with tears, saw Jesus. He looked deep into her eyes, reaching down to her soul and said, "Don't cry."

Can't you just feel these tender words coming from a

man who felt her pain, knew her despair, and realized her anxiety, stress, and worry?

Remember, Jesus knew what she was going through. He felt the pain of loss when his earthly father, Joseph, died.

He watched his mother grieve. He felt her pain and watched her suffer. He wiped her tears and listened to her spoken words tell of her broken heart. He knew the depth of pain she was feeling. He experienced it.

Jesus also knew this woman's situation was worse than his mother's. As the oldest son, he took over the carpentry business and provided for his family. This woman did not have any other son. She was all alone. She was destitute.

Then he went up and touched the bier they were carrying him on, and the bearers stood still. He said, "Young man, I say to you, get up!" The dead man sat up and began to talk, and Jesus gave him back to his mother (Luke 7:14–15).

I love the way that reads: **He gave him back to his mother.** Jesus' mercy and compassion reached out to her.

He raised her son from the dead.

He gave her son back to her.

He healed her broken heart.

He provided for her needs.

That day, a poor, lowly widow had a personal encounter with Jesus Christ. She experienced and witnessed his unexplainable power. He took time and personally intervened in her situation. That day he not only brought her son back to life, but he restored her life, too. He took away her grief and gave her hope. He moved heaven and earth for her—a widow.

Jesus took away her grief and gave her hope.

This isn't the only time we see Jesus intervening to help a widow. In Matthew 8:14–15, we read of Jesus healing Peter's mother-in-law from a desperately high fever. We can assume that since she was living at Peter's house, she, too, was a widow, dependant on her daughter and son-in-law. However, on this day, even they couldn't help her.

When Jesus came into Peter's house, he saw Peter's mother-in-law lying in bed with a fever. He touched her hand and the fever left her, and she got up and began to wait on him.

Peter was one of Jesus' disciples. Day after day, he was by Jesus' side watching as he healed the sick, delivered people from demons, and taught God's ways of living. This particular day Jesus was going to Peter's house for dinner. Probably exhausted from a long day, they were eager to get home, eat, and relax. Little did they know what was happening at the house.

When they arrived at Peter's house, his wife was frantic. She explained to everyone her mother was very sick with a high fever. She was scared because her mother was so sick she took to her bed. She didn't know what to do. She couldn't leave the family and go find them. She didn't know where to look for them. She was faced with this illness that could take her mother's life.

Peter, frightened and anxious, asked Jesus to go and pray for her. He had seen Jesus heal the sick for many days. Now his family needed a miracle from Jesus.

Jesus lovingly entered the sick woman's room. He took her hand, rebuked the fever and healed her. She went from being seriously ill to shedding tears of gratefulness. With one touch and a few words he healed her. He took away her suffering and pain. He cleared away her confusing thoughts that came with the high fever. He was there to meet the need that no one else could. Again, the object of his attention was a widow.

Overcome with gratitude, Peter's mother-in-law could hardly wait to repay Jesus for his love, kindness to her, and the compassion he showed her. Not having much that she could call her own, her immediate response was to get up and do something for him. She needed to show him how much she loved him. So she did what she could do: she prepared the meal so these famished men could eat. A woman who just moments before was facing eternity, was now serving food to the King of eternity—all because Jesus had compassion on an elderly widow.

The next passage where we see Jesus interacting with a widow is in Luke 21. However, we can't really say that he was interacting with her. He was actually observing her and holding her up as an example of true religion as he taught his disciples.

As Jesus looked up, he saw the rich putting their gifts into the temple treasury. He also saw a poor widow put in two very small copper coins (Luke 21:1–2).

Jesus and his disciples were once again in the temple at Jerusalem. From where they were standing, ironically in the court of the women, they could see many different types of people putting their offerings into the temple coffers. For some people, this was quite a production—especially if they were rich. Dressed in their finest attire, they wanted everyone to see how much of their wealth they were giving God. Oh, the show they put on as they dropped their gifts into the temple treasury, making sure everyone saw and appreciated their generosity. Then they walked away, quite proud of themselves, and went back to their normal lives.

However, as Jesus watched the parade of the rich, one by one, placing a portion of their wealth into the treasury, he wasn't impressed. So what? They had plenty more where that came from. More importantly, he knew their hearts and that they were more interested in impressing the crowds than pleasing God. Although their entrance may have been grand and their gift large, theirs was not the gift that made an impression on Jesus.

Instead, he was impressed with a woman who at first glance appeared to have given a very insignificant amount. Next to their grand attire, her widow's mourning clothes and weary appearance made it obvious she was poor. Her offering wouldn't impress anyone—in fact, it might be ridiculed.

After all, her two small copper coins were the smallest offering allowed to be given to the temple. To most, it seemed a pittance, but for her it was a sacrifice. It was all she could scrape together, all she had to live on for that day. To her, it was everything. But it was her heart's desire to give an offering to God, so she saved and sacrificed, knowing that God knew her situation. Still, she hoped no one noticed.

However, someone did notice. The most important "someone" noticed her. Because of his enormous sensitivity and compassion, Jesus didn't embarrass her by speaking to her or drawing public attention to her. She didn't need that— her offering was a gift between her and God. It was their moment and she would be rewarded in heaven.

Then, turning to his disciples, Jesus taught them a very important lesson.

"Truly I tell you," he said, "this poor widow has put in more than all the others. All these people

gave their gifts out of their wealth; but she out of her poverty put in all she had to live on" (Luke 21:3–4).

In a very private discussion, he used her gift to teach us all. Although she thought she escaped unnoticed, Jesus saw and he explained the significance of her gift.

You see, Jesus knew what the average onlooker didn't know. He knew that the man she had loved and shared her life with had died. He knew her husband did not leave her in a good financial state. In fact, he left her with very little. Now on top of her grief and loneliness, she had the harsh realities of poverty. Her life was hard. Still, she wanted to present her offering to God.

As he taught his disciples, Jesus did more than just tell them the facts about her life. He showed them what was in her heart. Because as we all know, **"The Lord does not look at the things people look at. People look at the outward appearance, but the Lord looks at the heart" (1 Samuel 16:7).**

Just what did Jesus see inside of her heart? He saw a woman who deeply loved God. She loved him so much that she wanted to give him a gift to show him her love. Like a small child who brings his mom a present to say "I love you," this woman brought her gift to God. That gift took great sacrifice on her part, but the sacrifice was overcome by the joy she felt at being able to show God that she loved him. What a tremendous love Jesus saw inside of her!

He also saw that this woman had great faith. Here was a woman who had so little, but she knew she could rely on God to provide for her needs. She knew she could depend on him, even when she had no one else to depend on. Having lost so much and having so little, she had every reason to have "trust issues," especially with God. Yet her actions show a faith and trust in God that defies reason.

As Jesus watched this woman, he saw faithfulness and loyalty in her heart. She had many reasons to be bitter and resentful at how her life turned out. She could have become angry with God that her husband died and she was alone. It would be understandable if she became resentful and jealous that she didn't have the financial security other women had. Each hour of her hard, lonely life gave her a reason to feel sorry for herself and be angry with God.

However, this wasn't the road she chose. Instead of running from God, she ran toward him. She accepted that God allowed these things in her life and she depended on him to help her through them. As she gave her gift, she proved that no matter what happened in her life, she would remain faithful to God and committed to him.

Inside of this woman's heart, Jesus saw strength. He saw strength that can only come from a personal relationship with God. It was a strength that went beyond understanding because it came directly from God and her reliance on him. How else could she find the courage to give all that she had?

This woman had a heart full of passion. She wasn't playing religion like so many others who were in the temple that day. She didn't give God a part of her life—she gave him everything. Here was a heart that was so passionate in her love for God and her relationship with him that she didn't hold anything back. She was completely sold out in her commitment to her heavenly Father.

When Jesus looked at her, he looked beyond her appearance and the amount of money she gave, and he saw her heart. It was the admirable qualities that he found there that he praised and saw as valuable. Jesus saw she was giving all she had to God out of a heart of love. He said that her gift was the greatest gift of all.

You see, one of the beautiful things about Jesus is that he sees beyond what others see. As we said before, Jesus knew up close and personal how difficult it was to be a widow. When Joseph died, Jesus accepted his responsibility as the oldest son and took over the carpentry business to help Mary provide for their family.

Although the Bible doesn't focus on these years in Jesus' life, it's important for us to remember that he lived them. In these years before entering the public ministry, Jesus lived a normal life with his very normal family. Because he experienced life as a working man, supporting his mom and his family, he has a keen understanding of people, relationships, and real life. He got an up-close and personal look at the life of a single mom when Joseph died and Mary was left alone. He understands the pain of grief, because he experienced losing his earthly father, Joseph. Because of these "silent" years in his life, he can understand the struggles, emotions, and challenges facing so many women today.

In his heart, you are a valuable treasure. You are not alone—he has not abandoned you!

Just as he did over two thousand years ago, Jesus has a special place in his heart for widows and orphans. Personally, I believe that in a society where men are so quick to throw off their responsibilities and abandon their wives and children, Jesus' empathy and concern extends to women who have been abandoned, divorced, or abused. Because of the circumstances he lived in while he walked the earth, he understands what you are going through. He is familiar with the heartache, the struggles, and the grief. He is there for you, just as he was for widows in the Bible two thousand years ago.

He knows what you're going through isn't easy. He sees as your heart breaks for your children and the dad who isn't in their lives. He feels your own heartache, as you wonder, "Why wasn't I enough? What was wrong with me that he chose to leave?" Jesus is there on the nights when you feel all alone. He's watching over you and your children, being the protector and provider that you need.

You are significant to him. In his heart, you are a valuable treasure. You are not alone—he has not abandoned you. He is walking beside you every step of the way, giving you strength, courage, and wisdom, even while he holds your heart in the palm of his hands. You can rely on him. He will be there for you. He speaks to you the words of Isaiah 54:4–5,

> **Do not be afraid; you will not be put to shame. Do not fear disgrace; you will not be humiliated. You will forget the shame of your youth and remember no more the reproach of your widowhood. For your Maker is your husband—the Lord Almighty is his name—the Holy One of Israel is your Redeemer; he is called the God of all the earth.**

Jesus also wants you to know that he sees your heart. In this world that is consumed by outward appearances and keeping up with the Joneses, Jesus sees the hearts of each and every widow, single mom, and abandoned woman who is doing her absolute best to serve him and raise her children to serve him. Just like he praised the poor widow at the temple for giving all she had, he is pleased at your dedication to giving him all you have.

As he did with her, he sees the challenges you face and the obstacles you've overcome. He knows you are trying to be both mom and dad, financial provider and emotional supporter. He sees it all. The one who sees it all knows you are pouring your heart and soul into serving him, remaining true to him despite the obstacles, raising your kids to serve him, and living your life according to his principles. Just as Jesus beamed with pride as he watched the poor widow deposit her offering into the coffers, he beams with pride over you and says, "That's my daughter! I'm so proud of her!"

Chapter 11 Questions

1. How do you think Mary's experience as a widow shaped Jesus' heart toward women?

2. Which woman can you identify with in this chapter?

3. How did this chapter encourage you on your own journey?

4. How can women who may not be grieving adopt Jesus' attitude and minister to women and their children who are grieving?

Chapter 12

The Thief on the Cross

We don't know much about him. Was he young or old? Married or single? Jewish or Roman? The Bible doesn't say much about him at all.

The only thing we really know about him for sure is that he was a thief—a criminal—a man on the wrong side of the law. We're not granted the full details of his crime. All the Bible chooses to tell us is that on the night Jesus was crucified, **"Two other men, both criminals, were also led out with him to be executed" (Luke 23:32).**

Whatever he did must have been pretty horrendous because his punishment was death by the cruelest and most torturous method known in Roman times.

Unlike Jesus' trial, his wasn't a speedy, overnight, behind-closed-doors trial on trumped-up charges. No, he really did what they said he did. When the "guilty" verdict came down, he wasn't even shocked. He knew it was exactly what he deserved.

The only thing he dared to wish for was that his execution wouldn't be by crucifixion. Death was one thing, but the thought of a cross was more than he could bear. With everything in him, he wished he would be executed by fire, stoned, or killed with the sword. Perhaps he'd be condemned to drink hemlock and die—anything but crucifixion.

Crucifixion was the most horrible death a man could die in the Roman Empire.

Crucifixion was the most horrible, agonizing, humiliating, painful death that any man could ever imagine. The thief felt like his head was going to explode when he heard "DEATH BY CRUCIFIXION."

Then there were the long, agonizing days of waiting for it to happen. They were filled with dread, fear, panic, and perhaps even a little bit of regret. Finally, the hour arrived and the soldiers came to begin the torture. It was his day to die. It was time.

Have you ever wondered at what point during this process the other thieves noticed Jesus?

I mean, I don't know what the average Roman crucifixion was like, but you would have to assume that this time was unique. All of the focus seemed to be on one man: Jesus.

It was an odd kind of attention. Yes, everyone expected the crowds of people to be hurling insults and hatreds at the criminals. However, there appeared to be a remnant of people who were sympathizing, even grieving with this man.

As the soldiers led him away, they seized Simon from Cyrene, who was on his way in from the country, and put the cross on him and made him carry it behind Jesus. A large number of people followed him, including women who mourned and wailed for him. Jesus turned and said to them, "Daughters of Jerusalem, do not weep for me; weep for yourselves and for your children. For the time will come when you will say, 'Blessed are the childless women, the wombs that never bore

and the breasts that never nursed!' Then "'they will say to the mountains, "Fall on us!" and to the hills, "Cover us!"' For if people do these things when the tree is green, what will happen when it is dry?" (Luke 23:26–31).

Did the thief hear Jesus comforting these women despite the excruciating, exhausting pain in his own body? What kind of man does this?

I mean, if anyone knew the pain Jesus was enduring, it was this guy—he was experiencing the same thing. Why wasn't Jesus angry? Why wasn't he cursing God and everyone? How could he find the strength to speak so kindly to these women and say, "Don't weep for me, but weep for yourselves?" There was definitely something strange about this man.

Perhaps the thief started watching Jesus when they were both hanging on the cross. **"When they came to the place called the Skull, they crucified him there, along with the criminals—one on his right, the other on his left." (Luke 23:33).**

Perhaps he saw that Jesus was no ordinary man when he was able to think beyond his own suffering to see that John would provide for his mother.

Near the cross of Jesus stood his mother, his mother's sister, Mary the wife of Clopas, and Mary Magdalene. When Jesus saw his mother there, and the disciple whom he loved standing nearby, he said to her, "Woman, here is your son," and to the disciple, "Here is your mother." From that time on, this disciple took her into his home (John 19:25–27).

No ordinary thief who deserved to be hung on a cross would do something like this. He wouldn't be worried about who took care of his mother. An ordinary man would only be able to think of himself at this time. Yet here was Jesus, making arrangements with his disciple and cousin, John, to make sure that Mary had a home. Who was this guy?

What did the sign, "King of the Jews" hanging over his head mean? Why was it written in so many languages?

Pilate had a notice prepared and fastened to the cross. It read: Jesus of Nazareth, the King of the Jews. Many of the Jews read this sign, for the place where Jesus was crucified was near the city, and the sign was written in Aramaic, Latin and Greek. The chief priests of the Jews protested to Pilate, "Do not write 'The King of the Jews,' but that this man claimed to be king of the Jews."

Pilate answered, "What I have written, I have written" (John 19:19–22).

Exactly who was this man hanging beside him?

If all of these things didn't show the thief Jesus' true identity, it must have been these words of Jesus: Jesus said, **"Father, forgive them, for they do not know what they are doing" (Luke 23:34).**

Even as:

And they divided up his clothes by casting lots.

The people stood watching, and the rulers even sneered at him. They said, "He saved others; let him save himself if he is God's Messiah, the Chosen One."

The soldiers also came up and mocked him. They offered him wine vinegar and said, "If you are the king of the Jews, save yourself" (Luke 23:34–38).

Even as all of this was happening, Jesus said, "Father, forgive them."

It had to be at this point that the thief realized what the centurion eventually said, **"Truly this was the Son of God"** **(Matthew 27:54 KJV).**

Just then, the other criminal being crucified with them decided to join in with the crowd. **"One of the criminals who hung there hurled insults at him: 'Aren't you the Messiah? Save yourself and us!'" (Luke 23:39).**

Was he serious? Couldn't he see that Jesus was different from them? They deserved to be there. They committed their crimes—in a sense, they earned their punishment. Couldn't he see that Jesus was innocent?

Not only was he innocent, but he really was who he claimed to be: the Messiah sent from God. There was no other explanation for his behavior, for his love, his concern for others, his lack of animosity, and his forgiveness.

But the other criminal rebuked him. "Don't you fear God?" he said, "since you are under the same sentence? We are punished justly, for we are getting what our deeds deserve. But this man has done nothing wrong" (Luke 23:40–41).

It's like he was saying, "Dude, we are about to die! Aren't you afraid of God's judgment at all? Are you seriously adding blasphemy to the list of crimes when we're about to face the Ultimate Judge? Can't you see that this man isn't like us? He's innocent. We're guilty. Are you seriously about to enter into eternity cursing the Messiah?"

Then the thief made a bold move. Then he said, **"Jesus, remember me when you come into your kingdom."**

This man knew what he was. He'd just confessed to the other criminal that he was a criminal. He was a sinner. He knew he deserved the punishment he was getting. Still, he dared to come to Jesus and ask for the same forgiveness that he's just seen Jesus give to those who were crucifying him.

That's when Jesus, hanging on the cross in excruciating physical, mental, and emotional pain, recognized significant faith in an insignificant sinner and said, **"Truly I tell you, today you will be with me in paradise" (Luke 23:43).**

This was an extraordinary moment. The first conversion under the new covenant happened to a thief while he was hanging on a cross.

The first conver-sion under the new covenant happened to a thief while he was hanging on a cross.

At this time, in both Roman and Jewish culture, there was no one more insignificant, more despised, more unworthy than a criminal experiencing crucifixion. Such a man was even seen as being cursed by God. Trust me, there was no minister going into the Roman prison trying to convert this man before his execution. He was seen as the scum of the earth—destined not only to a torturous death, but to an eternity of suffering for his sins.

However, even in his own weak state of consuming pain, Jesus took a moment to see this man's significance as a human being. It wasn't because of anything the man did or would ever be able to do in Christ's kingdom. This man's life was over.

No, Jesus simply saw his value as a human, eternal soul. Jesus heard his repentant heart. Like he'd done for so many other insignificant, unclean sinners, Jesus forgave him and offered him a place in his kingdom.

The thief's life may have ended that day, but his future was just beginning. Within hours, that man was no longer a condemned sinner, but he was a child of God welcomed into heaven because Christ bore his sin on the cross. When he asked for Christ's forgiveness, he received a new life, a new identity, and new hope for eternity.

While the religious leaders rejoiced that they had fulfilled their mission and saved the Jewish religion from a deceptive heretic, Jesus was still doing the work of his Father and bringing lost sheep into the fold.

At a time when it would have been easy to focus on himself—his pain, his mistreatment, and his sacrifice—he was still focused on the needs of those around him. From the cross, he still reached out to the least of these and offered them the kingdom of heaven.

Even during his crucifixion, Jesus was still fulfilling his mission: **To seek and save those who are lost.**

Even today, the same hope that was offered to the thief on the cross is available to every man, woman, and child that will recognize who Jesus is, his or her own need for a Savior, and turn to him in repentance. In Jesus' eyes, no one is too far gone, too guilty, or too big of a sinner. In God's heart, no one is too wretched to receive forgiveness and become a part of his family. Each and every person has significance as an eternal soul. Because he sees this value, God's invitation is always open, the question is: Will you turn to him, like the thief on the cross? Will you repent and enter a new kingdom—the kingdom of God?

Chapter 12 Questions

1. This man reached out to Jesus because he saw something different in Jesus—how he acted. Was there someone in your life whose different life led you to Jesus?

2. Has there been anyone who has seen a difference in your life and come to Jesus?

3. If not, what needs to change in your life?

4. In his most difficult time in life, Jesus' focus was still on helping others, not himself. Can you say the same thing about your life? Would others say this about your life?

5. What changes do you need to make to ensure this would be your legacy?

Chapter 13

Peter—The Story of a Failure

Failure.

℣t was as if that word was pounding in Peter's head as he recalled the events of the past few days. How could he have failed so miserably? Then he began to recall...

When Jesus hung on the cross, he was hardly recognizable. He was badly beaten and bruised. His body was covered in his own blood. You could see his skeleton through his torn and shattered skin. They had beaten him so badly.

One may not have known he was Jesus—but Peter knew. He knew those eyes. Sure, his eyes were swollen, bruised, and discolored, but Peter knew they belonged to Jesus. How could he ever forget those eyes?

They are the eyes which three years earlier had looked at him and called him to be a disciple. They're the eyes that shined with laughter as he joked with Peter. Those eyes had been filled with pride when Peter proudly proclaimed Jesus was the Son of God. Those same eyes looked through Simon and his past, and renamed him Peter, the rock, the man he had the potential to be.

Many times Jesus' eyes gave a little roll when Peter made one of his famously idiotic statements. Those eyes burned with holy anger when Jesus threw the money changers out of the temple. Those eyes shone with the glory of God on the Mount of Transfiguration.

Peter saw love and compassion in Jesus' eyes as he ministered to the sick and the needy. Those same eyes turned in a stinging rebuke to Peter when he told Jesus not speak of his death. Just days earlier, the same eyes filled with tears as Jesus wept over the city of Jerusalem. Those were Jesus' eyes—they were the eyes of Peter's best friend.

As Peter looked upon Jesus on the cross, his own eyes filled with tears. While those eyes have portrayed all those things to Peter, this is not what Peter was thinking about. He was thinking of how in the past twenty-four hours, he had betrayed his closest and dearest friend.

"He warned me! Why didn't I listen?"

This was true; Jesus had warned Peter that he was to undergo a satanic attack. Jesus knew that an all-out affront on the kingdom of God was about to commence. As the forces of evil prepared to destroy Jesus, Satan also requested to take his best shot at Peter, the man Jesus had appointed to lead the church after he was gone.

Jesus warned Peter of the coming attack.

"Why didn't I listen?" Peter must have thought. "I was so confident that I could withstand it. I would die with Jesus if need be; but I would never, ever turn my back on him."

This was the attitude that opened Peter up to the attack. It was the Simon in him, the old man, which caused his downfall. Little did he know that this was why God allowed

Satan to attack him. Satan needed to kill Simon so Peter could become all that God wanted him to be. But as Peter looked at Jesus on the cross, he didn't know this. All he knew was that he had failed.

"He warned me to pray for strength," Peter surely thought. And this was true. In the Garden of Gethsemane, a place where Jesus often went, Jesus warned Peter to pray so he wouldn't give in to temptation.

In his cocky ignorance Peter didn't pray. He slept. Jesus kept waking him, but Peter kept falling back asleep. That is, until they came.

Peter was awakened by an angry mob of people. They came ready to fight. They were here to arrest Jesus; how dare they! No one messes with Peter's best friend. He quickly drew his sword and swung at the man nearest him, attempting to cut off his head, but instead the sword severed his ear.

At that point, Jesus' eyes burned as he turned to Peter and told him to put away his sword. Peter was dumbfounded as Jesus took the severed ear and restored it to the man.

Peter did not realize that this was the last miracle he would see Jesus perform before his death. He did not understand that no blood but Jesus' blood could be shed that night. All he knew that was Jesus was in trouble.

As the angry mob led Jesus away, Peter faithfully followed behind them. At first he had run away, but now he was following secretly behind the angry crowd. He needed to somehow help his best friend. How, he did not know, but help he must. Little did he know he was not just following Jesus. The Simon in him was preparing to enter the wheat sifter.

The mob led Jesus into the courtyard of the high priest for his trial, and Peter followed. At first, Peter couldn't get inside, but John, his good friend and fellow disciple, had also followed Jesus. Since John had connections with the high priest, he got someone to let Peter enter. Peter went to a fire to get warm and see what would happen.

How could Peter stand to be around the very people who were cursing and reviling Jesus? What business did he have with them? He had been warned by Jesus that Satan was after him. Did he not realize that this was not just a fire to warm him? It was the opening Satan needed for the fierce attack about to be leveled against Peter. Now it will begin.

As Peter warned himself, he noticed a girl at the door looking at him. "This man was with him," she said.

Peter had been discovered. Now what? Maybe he thought, What good could he do for Jesus if he was captured, too?

In a panic, he said, "Girl, I don't know him."

Without realizing what he had done, a panicking Simon, (for this was certainly not the behavior of a Peter, a rock) quickly got up and made his way to a balcony. Satan had successfully delivered his first blow to Peter.

Peter moved to the balcony to avoid the notice of the people, but to no avail. "He was with him," a voice proclaimed.

Peter stopped dead in his tracks.

"I am not with him," Peter insisted.

Deeper and further into sin and denial went Peter. It was getting easier to speak the lie. The words were coming out easier than at first.

Peter was knee deep in the wheat sifter. Satan was slowly showing the world that Peter was no rock. He was an ordinary man. He cared for no one but himself. He wasn't about to pick up a cross and follow Jesus. He would never surrender himself for the good of the kingdom.

Church world, behold the man who was picked to lead you after Jesus! If he betrayed Jesus, what would he do to them? There was no Peter...there was Simon.

Satan prepared for the final blow. He was about to finish Simon off. About an hour later, Peter ran into the cousin of the man whose ear he had cut off. "You were with him," the man proclaimed. Peter had had enough. "By the name of God, I did not know him!"

Then Peter proclaimed a few expletives to prove his point. At that moment, the rooster crowed. Peter stopped in his tracks and looked at Jesus, only to meet those eyes staring back at him.

One look from Jesus told Peter everything he needed to know. Best friends have a way of doing this. They can look at each other and know what the other is thinking.

Did Jesus' look portray hurt, disgust, an I-told-you-so look?

Was it a look of sympathy? Did it say, "I know you have fallen under Satan's hand"? Was it a look of love and understanding?

More than likely, it was a tender and compassionate look, a look of mingled affection, pity, and reproof. Whatever the look, it pierced Peter, "the rock," and shattered him into tiny pebbles. He was broken. But much to Satan's dismay, something remained...a small grain of faith, for Peter immediately repented.

Sobbing and beating his chest, he begged God for forgiveness. He knew true conviction, shame, heart sorrow, and he begged God for a new start.

Jesus' look brought all of Jesus' words back to Peter. Included in those words was **"When you have repented...."** He was going to do this. He had to make things right, for as he had said months before to Jesus, "Where else do I have to go?"

Peter sought forgiveness.

Now a few hours later Peter was standing there by the cross. Tears wet his cheeks again as he stood before Jesus on the cross.

Jesus' eyes now seemed less lifelike. Peter's best friend slowly and painfully fought to speak.

"It is finished" Jesus proclaimed in a voice which was unusually strong for a man in his physical condition. Then he closed his eyes and died.

Peter wept.

Jesus was dead. He never got a chance to make it right. The last intimate moment he spent with his best friend was a moment that in Peter's eyes severed the relationship. Those last three words burned in his heart. He thought, "He is gone, and it truly is finished."

But was it?

Fast-forward a few days. It was the dawn of a new day in Galilee. The early morning rays of light crept up over the horizon. The early morning sunlight revealed a sign hung on the door of a house. It was Peter's house. The sign read "Gone Fishin'." Peter was back to the sea. He needed to get away to think, to clear his head, to mull over the events of the past few weeks.

As he and a few of the other disciples fished, Peter's thoughts went back over all the ups and downs of the past few weeks. Constantly before him was fact that he had denied Jesus.

This was the second-lowest point of it all. It still broke his heart as he remembered the eyes of Jesus, which both gently rebuked and at the same time expressed the great love he had for Peter.

His eyes still filled with tears as he heard daily the sound of a rooster crowing. Then there was the lowest point of it all—when he had watched Jesus die. He felt the wrenching pain of loss, the loneliness, the heartache. For days he wept the loss of his best friend.

Then, early Sunday morning, Mary came running to him with a message. She excitedly and a bit hysterically announced Jesus was alive! She claimed he'd spoken to her and told her to go and tell the others—especially Peter—that he was alive.

Peter didn't know what to think. His logic told him it was impossible, yet his heart burned with hope and excitement within him. He had to know. For the first time since Jesus died his denial of Jesus was not the only thing on his mind. He wanted to see Jesus. He wanted to see his best friend.

Off he ran toward the tomb with his good friend, John. John, who had always been faster than Peter, ran ahead. As Peter ran full speed toward the tomb, he thought, "Could it really be true?"

As they came to the tomb they found exactly what Mary had told them. John stood at the entrance looking at the tomb, but in true Peter form, Peter walked right in and examined the contents. The grave clothes were exactly as they had been, but they were hollow! No body was wrapped inside. The head cover was neatly folded. No man could have stolen the body without disturbing the grave clothes. It must be true. Jesus must have risen!

Not long after this, Peter and the other disciples were all meeting together. Some were afraid of the Pharisees, so the doors were locked. All of a sudden, Jesus appeared among them! He was alive! Peter was face to face with Jesus.

Jesus calmed all of their fears by showing them he truly was alive and not a ghost. He even ate some fish with them.

Then he took them step by step through the Old Testament and showed them all the prophecy he had fulfilled. He even answered the doubts of Thomas by letting him feel his hands and feet. It was true—Jesus really was alive.

As Peter remembered these things, a tear fell from his eye. It was dried by the cool sea breeze, but Peter didn't notice. His mind drifted back to his last meeting with Jesus. Peter had plenty of time to mull all of this over, for they had not caught a fish the whole time. Little did he know he is about to relive a memory from a few years earlier.

"Have you caught anything?" a voice from shore yelled out.

"No," came the reply from the group of tired fishermen.

"Throw your net to the other side of the boat," the voice replied.

A bit of déjà vu was happening here. They obediently threw the net to the other side. Instantly, it was full of fish. John was the first to realize what was going on. "It is the Lord!" he excitedly exclaimed.

That was all Peter needed to hear. He quickly grabbed his coat and in true Peter fashion jumped out of the boat and into the water. He had to be near Jesus.

Since they weren't far from the shore, all of the disciples in the boat arrived at the same time as Peter. They arrived to find Jesus had built a fire and had already prepared some fish and bread for them. They ate together, just like old times. Jesus truly was alive.

Peter had to be near Jesus!

After the meal, Jesus asked Peter to take a walk with him. Knowing all things, Jesus knew Peter was in need of some attention. He had a wound deep in his heart, and Jesus was going to operate on him to heal him.

Turning to Peter, Jesus said "Peter, do you love me and are you willing to sacrifice yourself out of love for me even more than these?"

With the hands of a skilled physician, Jesus made his first incision. Peter understood what Jesus was doing. He was making Peter remember the bold profession he had made just before he denied Jesus.

When Jesus had predicted his denial, Peter proudly proclaimed, "Even if all men are offended by you, I'll never be offended."

The healing was under way. Jesus was making Peter face his sin. Peter had to look at his heart. An answer had to be made.

"Lord, you know I love you."

Peter was not about to bring the others into it. He loved Jesus, but he had denied him. Peter was well aware of his faults now. Any aura of pride was gone. Peter knew he was no better than anyone else.

Jesus knew this too, for he said to Peter, "Feed my sheep."

Peter was to furnish food for the souls of the believers to come. The pus in Peter's infected heart was being removed. It was time for the next incision.

"Simon, do you truly love me?" Jesus asked. He was saying, "Simon, do you love me ardently and supremely?"

Peter, knowing enough not to rely on his own heart, thoughts, feelings, and emotions again appealed to his all knowing Savior and said, "Lord, you know I have love for you."

Peter was not going to fall into a trap of pride and conceit again. Jesus was going to have to see inside of him to know that he loved him, for Jesus knew his heart better than anyone, even Peter.

Jesus said to Peter, "Feed my sheep."

He was charging him to be faithful in caring for and guiding the future believers. Peter's heart was now ready for the final incision.

"Peter, are you my friend?" The incision was made, the pus revealed. Jesus had a way of getting to the heart of the matter. Peter had denied Jesus three times. Jesus now gave him a chance three times to proclaim his allegiance to Jesus and re-instate their deep friendship.

Remember, this was not an attack to show Peter his guilt. Jesus had already appeared to Peter and expressed his forgiveness. This was about making Peter face his past and forgive himself so that he could become the rock that Jesus had called him to be. Peter had been humbled, and Jesus was showing him how he had been humbled, how it had affected his mind, and how it had prepared him for the future ministry.

"Are you my friend?" The words cut straight to Peter's heart. There it was. He had to face himself.

Three times he had denied his best friend. He knew it. Jesus knew it. Peter's faults were out in the open. He had to face it. He had to be made aware that he had fallen. The past had to be dealt with before there could be a future.

"Jesus, you know I love you," was the reply from the broken-hearted Peter. And this was true. He did love Jesus.

Jesus went on to show Peter why these things had to be addressed. He was still Jesus' man. Jesus still believed in him. He was still the right man for the job. But Peter had to know that it was not his own strength, his own passion, or his own feelings that would endure the future struggles. It could only be done through Jesus. Peter knew that in himself he would fail, so he had to rely on Jesus and his strength. In his weakness, Jesus would make him strong.

Jesus was once again calling him to follow him. The impetuous Simon would no longer jump ahead and do things in his own power. Peter, the rock, would follow behind Jesus, knowing that without Jesus, the rock could easily be smashed into pebbles.

From that moment on, Peter, through the power of the Holy Spirit, became the most firm and unwavering of all the apostles. He was the rock that the church was founded on. He preached boldly, bringing thousands to Christ after Pentecost. He boldly proclaimed the truth before the leaders who just months before he hid from in a locked house.

He endured prison, beatings, the murder of his wife on the cross before his very eyes, and even his own death upon the cross. He was able to do it all because of his love and dependence on Jesus, his best friend.

Because Jesus didn't give up on Peter, even when he failed, even when he denied him, Peter was able to once again find his significance in Christ. After finding his significance in Christ, Peter was finally able to become the man Jesus always intended him to be and fill his role in Jesus' kingdom.

Just as he did for Peter, Jesus offers forgiveness for your failures.

This same hope is available to all who are reading this and hearing the word "Failure" ring through their brain. Just as he did for Peter, Jesus offers forgiveness for your failures. He wants to heal your broken heart, and restore your relationship with him.

The amazing thing about Jesus is that even when we fail, Jesus doesn't throw us away. He doesn't give up and say, "You're finished." Peter's life proves that there is hope for failures. Just as Jesus was able to take Peter's failures and use them to make Peter an even more effective minister for him, Jesus will do the same for you.

I want to encourage you. No matter what mistakes or sins you have committed, there is hope and restoration through Jesus. All he asks is that you humbly come to him and allow him to do work inside of you. You have to be willing to face your sin, and allow God to change you, to heal your heart, change your thinking, and teach you how to live in his kingdom.

Once you spend time getting healing for your issues, God can lift you up out of the mess you made of your life and use you to help set someone else free who is living in the same situation. Once Peter allowed God to change him, he was used mightily by God to help others. The same will happen with you. You will help others through the power of God, not through any strength of your own. Your failures can lead to your greatest success once you allow God to work on your heart and set you free.

Allow God to begin today.

Chapter 13 Questions

1. Have you ever felt like you failed God so badly that there was no way to make it right?

2. What finally broke Peter? Was there an event in your life that broke you and caused you to come to the end of yourself?

3. Peter had a heart-to-heart chat with Jesus and allowed Jesus to expose and clean out the wounds in Peter's soul. Have you ever had an experience like this with Jesus?

4. This chapter makes clear that Peter couldn't start again after his failure until he dealt with the issue that caused him to fail. What is the root issue of your failure?

Chapter 14

Mary Magdalene— A Story of Hope

Strike one: She was a woman.
Strike two: She earned her living as a prostitute.
Strike three: She was controlled by seven demons.
Three strikes—you're out.

*M*ary Magdalene knew this mentality, prevalent in Jewish society, all too well.

To the religious leaders, she was a sinner. Unclean. They avoided her like the plague, fearful that her sins were contagious and would ruin their stellar reputations. They didn't see her as a soul in need of repentance. She was evil, and should be avoided. Mary was all too familiar with the pain of being an outcast.

Those who knew her personally, the family and friends she grew up with, gave up long ago. I'd imagine most people saw her as a hopeless individual—too many demons, too many problems, too much sin. What could be done? They looked at her the way we sometimes look at people. We say,

185

"Oh, that's just Mary. She's always been that way. She'll always be that way. Nobody knows what to do with her!"

For all intents and purposes, she was "out" of the game of life. Useless. What good could ever come from her? Then she met Jesus and everything changed. He offered her salvation from her sins, deliverance from the demons that were destroying her life, healing for the pain in her soul and mind, and a completely new life as a child of God.

Then came the day that she and the other women who were following Jesus were forced to stand by his cross and watch him die.

Some women were watching from a distance. Among them were Mary Magdalene, Mary the mother of James the younger and of Joseph, and Salome. In Galilee these women had followed him and cared for his needs. Many other women who had come up with him to Jerusalem were also there (Mark 15:40–41).

I wonder what Mary was thinking as she watched him die? She must have wondered if the end of his life would also mean the end of the freedom and hope she enjoyed. She couldn't imagine the thought of having to go back under the oppression in which she once lived. How do you go back to a life of solitude and torment when you have experienced the freedom that only Jesus could give?

Whatever her thoughts, they were interrupted by a cry from the cross. She looked upwards at the one to whom she owed her freedom. He cried out in a loud voice **"It Is finished."** Then he lowered his head and died.

Immediately, the forces in the heavenlies seemed to rage at a greater level than ever before as the sun went dark and the earth shook. Evil seemed to prevail.

Mary was heartbroken. The one she loved and served was dead. Freedom for the captives seemed gone forever. Mary thought it all was over with the cry, **"It is finished."** She didn't know it was just the beginning. All she knew was that he was gone and her heart was shattered.

Still, there was resilience about Mary and the other women who followed Jesus to the cross. They didn't abandon Jesus. Unlike the disciples who ran and Peter who denied him, they stood firm in their loyalty. In fact, it was the women who followed him beyond the cross into Resurrection Day.

Luke 23:55–56 reads,

The women who had come with Jesus from Galilee followed Joseph and saw the tomb and how his body was laid in it. Then they went home and prepared spices and perfumes. But they rested on the Sabbath in obedience to the commandment.

I think if we were honest, we really can't imagine what the days between the crucifixion and Sunday morning were like for these women. They had just witnessed the horrific, agonizing death of someone they loved, esteemed, and regarded as the Messiah. I'm sure sleep was impossible as the images of the previous day flashed through their minds, intermixed with the good memories of times spent with Jesus. They remembered him teaching the people, lovingly welcoming the little children, and healing the sick. Their grief must have been overwhelming!

Yet they prepared to do what they did best—as they'd taken care of him in life, they would prepare his body in death. Still, there was that long day of Sabbath before they could go to the tomb. For them, it had to be a day filled with tears, grief, shock, and horror.

Finally, dawn peeked through on Sunday morning. The long Sabbath was over, and the women prepared to go to the tomb. Luke 24:1–11 tells us their story.

On the first day of the week, very early in the morning, the women took the spices they had prepared and went to the tomb.

They found the stone rolled away from the tomb, but when they entered, they did not find the body of the Lord Jesus.

While they were wondering about this, suddenly two men in clothes that gleamed like lightning stood beside them.

I find it fascinating that the first people God chose to hear the good news of Christ's resurrection from the dead were the women who faithfully followed him and supported him while he was on earth.

In their fright the women bowed down with their faces to the ground, but the men said to them, "Why do you look for the living among the dead? He is not here; he has risen! Remember how he told you, while he was still with you in Galilee: 'The Son of Man must be delivered over to the hands of sinners, be crucified and on the third day be raised again.'" Then they remembered his words.

When they came back from the tomb, they told all these things to the Eleven and to all the others. It was Mary Magdalene, Joanna, Mary the

mother of James, and the others with them who told this to the apostles. But they did not believe the women, because their words seemed to them like nonsense.

I find it fascinating that the first people God chose to hear the good news of Christ's resurrection from the dead were the women who faithfully followed him and supported him while he was on earth!

Later, we read that the first person Jesus appeared to after his resurrection was Mary Magdalene. John 20:11–18,

Now Mary stood outside the tomb crying. As she wept, she bent over to look into the tomb and saw two angels in white, seated where Jesus' body had been, one at the head and the other at the foot.

They asked her, "Woman, why are you crying?"

"They have taken my Lord away," she said, "and I don't know where they have put him."

At this, she turned around and saw Jesus standing there, but she did not realize that it was Jesus.

He asked her, "Woman, why are you crying? Who is it you are looking for?"

Thinking he was the gardener, she said, "Sir, if you have carried him away, tell me where you have put him, and I will get him."

Jesus said to her, "Mary."

She turned toward him and cried out in Aramaic, "Rabboni!" (which means "Teacher").

Jesus said, "Do not hold on to Me, for I have not yet ascended to the Father. Go instead to my brothers and tell them, 'I am ascending to my Father and your Father, to my God and your God.'"

Mary Magdalene went to the disciples with the news: "I have seen the Lord!" And she told them that he had said these things to her.

Now I don't know about you, but if I were God, I think I might have been tempted to make another choice. If I were going to announce the greatest miracle in the history of the universe, I would want to write it in the sky for the whole world to see. "Death has lost its victory! Jesus has risen!"

Or maybe I might have started with the Roman government and announced, "You guys were wrong! You crucified an innocent man! Once more, he was no ordinary man—he is the Son of the only true and living God. Guess what? He's alive! Death couldn't hold him! The King of Kings and Lord of Lords rose from the dead to rule and reign for all eternity!"

Perhaps if I were Jesus, I'd have chosen to show up in the middle of the temple and scare the living daylights out of the religious rulers. I'd want them to see that all their scheming and attempts at assassination were just a part of God's plan. Maybe I'd want to prove to the Sadducees that there is a resurrection from the dead. For sure, I'd want them to know their plans hadn't worked, but Jesus had overcome and risen from the dead!

Possibly I'd take a softer approach and make my first appearance to my mom and my family—to comfort them and tell them I was okay. Maybe I'd make my first appearance to the disciples.

But God didn't choose any of these people to be the first to hear the news of Jesus' resurrection. Instead, God chose to make the greatest announcement in history to a group of virtually unknown women who were fully committed to loving and serving Jesus. Jesus made his first appearance in his resurrected body to a woman that many people had written off as hopeless. However, in Jesus, there is always hope.

Remember, before she met Jesus, Mary Magdalene wasn't what anyone would call a success story. She was a woman with many labels: Sinner. Failure. Demon-possessed. Hopeless. Useless. Unredeemable.

But that's not what Jesus saw when he met her. As he does with all of us, Jesus looked past Mary's problems and looked into her soul. When he looked into her soul, he saw the woman she was originally created to be. He also saw the circumstances that damaged her soul, and allowed entrance to the demons that were destroying her life.

Still, he didn't stop there. Because Jesus is God, he saw what he could do to change Mary. He saw the valuable treasure she could become for the kingdom of God.

Jesus offered Mary salvation from her sins, deliverance from the demons that were destroying her life, healing for the pain in her soul and mind, and a completely new life as a child of God. Ultimately, Jesus offered her the opportunity to be the first evangelist in New Testament history when he told her to go tell the disciples that he was alive.

What a difference—from a demonically controlled woman to an evangelist all because of what Jesus did in her life! This hope is what Jesus offers to every person who will come to him and accept him as the Savior and Lord of his or her life.

This is the reason there is hope for every woman on the

> No matter who or what is responsible for damaging your soul, Jesus wants to heal you!

planet. Like he did with Mary, when Jesus looks at you, he sees a woman whom he loves. As he did with Mary, he doesn't just look at the outward finished product.

When Jesus met Mary he didn't just see a woman possessed with seven demons. He saw a woman who had experienced something traumatic that had allowed those demons to enter her.

Obviously, we don't know what happened to her. Perhaps she was abused as a child or she was treated poorly in a relationship. Maybe she dabbled in the occult or chose to participate in sin that allowed these demons to enter. We don't know.

In the same way, I don't know what caused the pain and brokenness that is inside of you. However, I do know one thing. No matter who or what is responsible for damaging your soul, Jesus wants to heal you. Yes, he knows about your issues and your sin, but that's not all he knows. He knows why you are the way you are. He wants to offer you the same new life that he offered to Mary. He can give you hope—a chance to start over again.

The first thing Jesus wants to offer you is salvation from your sins.

The Bible says, **"All have sinned and fall short of the glory of God" (Romans 3:23).** This sin has separated us from God. In ourselves, there's nothing we can do to make our relationship with God right again. That's why Jesus came to earth.

Because he is God, he has never sinned. Because he is sinless, he was able to take the punishment of death that we deserve. It's not that God doesn't know we sinned or he's overlooking our sin. No, Jesus took the punishment for our sin. Because he took our punishment, our sins can be forgiven. We can experience salvation, we can enter into a personal relationship with God, and we are given the hope of eternal life in heaven.

But that isn't all Jesus wants to do to help you. After all, he did more for Mary. He didn't just forgive her sins and offer her the hope of eternal life. He changed her life here on earth.

Jesus is offering you the same thing—hope for a better life on earth. He wants to heal the pain and the damage inside of your mind, soul, and spirit, and he wants to deliver you from any demonic influences or generational iniquities from your past that are controlling your present and seeking to destroy your future.

I know some people hear this and say, "Why can't God love me the way I am?"

The answer is that God does love you the way you are. In fact, he loves you too much to let you stay that way. Honestly, what parent could look at a child with a broken arm and a dislocated leg, crying and in pain and say, "Oh honey, I accept you just the way you are, I'm not going to do anything to try to help you"?

That's not love! That's cruel! A loving parent would help his child and take her to the doctor. He would do everything he could to help the child heal, be free from pain, and be able to live life normally. That's love!

Recently, I went through a back injury. When I went into the doctor's office, I didn't want him to say, "Hey, Adessa, don't worry about it. I like you just the way you are, so I'm not going to realign your spine so you can stand up straight."

Truthfully, that's not what I wanted to hear. I wanted him to make the pain stop!

That's what Jesus wants to do for every woman who comes to him with a broken heart, damaged mind, or wounded spirit. He wants to bring healing, health, and wholeness.

All of us, no matter who we are, have souls that are damaged in one way or another. For better or for worse, the circumstances and people in our lives affect our souls, our self-images, our minds, and our views of life.

Many women are carrying the scars from damage their souls received when they were little girls or teenagers.

Other women's souls were wounded in bad relationships.

Some have experienced disappointments or heartaches.

Others have made choices that were wrong and caused damage to their own souls.

No matter what the circumstances, all of this damage accumulates and affects who we are. Eventually, the damage to our mind, soul, and personality keeps us from the purposes God designed for us.

That's why Jesus wants to heal the damage in your mind and soul from your past. He wants to help you overcome the unforgiveness and bitterness that are destroying you—not because he thinks the other person was right—but because he knows these things are killing your soul and he wants you to be free.

Jesus wants to set you free from your tendency toward accepting abuse or allowing yourself to be treated badly.

He wants to deliver you from your hot temper or your anger issues.

As he did for Mary, he wants to begin the process of changing you and making you into a holy, healthy woman, capable of being all God intended you to be.

Isaiah 53 says it this way, **"But he was pierced for our transgressions, he was crushed for our iniquities; the punishment that brought us peace was on him, and by his wounds we are healed."** This promise doesn't just apply to physical healing, but it applies to healing in our minds, souls, and emotions.

Along with healing you and delivering you, Jesus wants to teach you to live a new way. Again, we see that Mary wasn't just saved and delivered from demons, but her entire way of life changed. Whatever her life was before, she now had a new life as a follower of Christ. The same is possible for every woman when she comes to know Jesus as her Savior.

As Jesus heals your heart and mind, and as you spend time with him in prayer and Bible reading, you will begin to learn how to live in God's kingdom. The Holy Spirit will lead and guide you and teach you how God's kingdom principles can be applied to each and every area of your life. When you commit yourself to living by God's ways, you, too, will experience change.

Every day, the Holy Spirit will help you apply God's principles to your life. If you choose to obey God's principles, you will start to see that your life is different. You yourself will change.

With every hurt you allow God to heal and every choice you make to follow God's ways rather than sinful ways, you will be one step closer to becoming the strong, capable, spiritually healthy woman God designed you to be. That's what he did for Mary, and he wants to do the same thing for you.

That is the heart of all women's ministry. Jesus loves women. He loves them so much that he wants to offer them a place in his kingdom, just as he did Mary and the other women who went to the tomb.

For each of his daughters, God has a unique plan and purpose. When he looks at you he sees beyond what other people see, and he sees into your heart. He knew you from the time you were a baby inside of your mom. He watched you grow up. He laughed when you laughed and he cried when you cried. He knows every circumstance or person you've ever encountered in life. He's seen you win great victories and overcome difficult obstacles just to get to where you are today.

He knows the choices you've made—good and bad. He knows all about the sins in your life, the pain in your heart, and the damage in your soul. If we're honest, we know that even the most religious, perfect-appearing woman among us has struggles and issues inside.

Jesus knows everything about you and he still loves you. Today, he is reaching out to you saying, "Come to me and accept the help I want to give you. Because of what I did at Calvary I can give you forgiveness for your sins. Because of the blood I shed, I can offer you healing for your body, soul, mind, and spirit, and deliverance from all the sins, demons, and generational iniquities that hold you captive. Please, come to me and let me help you. Let me change you. Allow me the opportunity to heal your soul.

"Yes, it may hurt. Yes, it may not always be easy, but what healing is? Would you really avoid going to a doctor with a broken arm just because it might hurt having the arm put in a cast? No, you wouldn't. I'm the same way. Trust me. Everything I do is for your good.

"I want to do the same miracle inside of you that I did inside of Mary Magdalene. I want to offer you a new life, free from all the things that are holding you captive. As I am healing each issue, I will be right there walking beside you, holding you and making you healthy again. Please, allow me to do with you what I did with Mary. Let me offer you a new life and a new hope. I know what I have planned for you. I know what I designed you to be. I want you to be a strong, productive, capable woman that I can use in my kingdom."

That is the heart of Jesus reaching out to each one of us, offering us the hope of a new life of freedom and spiritual health in him. Just as everything changed on Easter, over two thousand years ago, so your life can be completely changed today.

Because of Jesus, there is hope—hope for salvation, hope for a new life, and hope for eternity. The question is: Will you, like Mary Magdalene, accept Jesus' offer of hope and submit your life completely to him? For her, answering "Yes" meant freedom from the past, change in the present, and a hope for the future. The same can be true for you.

Chapter 14 Questions

1. **Has anyone ever treated you like you "had too many problems, too much sin"?**

2. **Have you ever looked at other people this way?**

3. **What does** *hopeless* **look like to you?**

4. **How has Jesus brought you hope?**

5. **How can you help other women experience the same hope?**

Epilogue

"Follow me, and I will make you fishers of men."
"Go and sin no more."
"Take up your mat and walk."
"Your faith has made you well."

*T*hese were the words Jesus spoke to the people that the world called:

Ordinary.
Insignificant.
Unsophisticated.
Unredeemable.
Working Class.
Unimportant.
Worthless.

Still, no matter what label the world had placed on them, the Master spoke words of significance and purpose into their lives. Ultimately, his entrance into their lives changed their entire identity.

A poor young couple from Nazareth became the earthly parents to the Son of God.

The shepherds were no longer outcasts when they were included in the birth of the Messiah.

Anna's grief ended when her eyes saw what they had waited so long to behold.

The wise men's paths and lives were rerouted.

Someone very, very good did come from the despised

town of Nazareth, as it became forever known as Jesus' hometown.

Not only did Jesus put the town of Nazareth on the map, but the entire region of Galilee. From this region, he chose some of the oddest misfits he could find, all with personal issues that had to be overcome. He taught them, trained them, lived with them, and mentored them. After three years with him, they became men of great faith who revolutionized the world as they spread the gospel of Jesus Christ.

From the very beginning of his ministry, Jesus caused a stir. Breaking the rules of the Jewish religious leaders to follow the Laws of God, Jesus ministered to Samaritans, foreigners, and the ceremonially unclean. Although the religious leaders were appalled, the hosts of heaven rejoiced when a promiscuous Samaritan woman became a child of God and evangelized her town. The heart of the heavenly Father rejoiced as Jesus fulfilled his desire and showed his love to the Gentiles.

Lepers were cleansed.

Demoniacs were set free and spread the news about Jesus.

Sinners were forgiven and started new lives.

Jesus spoke significance to the lives of women and children as he removed social barriers and cultural stigmas and offered them a place in his kingdom.

Where it appeared there was no hope, he became the hope they needed.

No one was too evil or too far gone to be deemed beyond his touch. As the thief on the cross learned, it's never too late to repent and become reconciled to God.

Jesus gave failures a second chance, and offered hope to lives that everyone else thought was hopeless.

Over and over again, throughout the New Testament, we see Jesus speaking salvation, healing, and new life into people's lives. Where it appeared there was no hope, he became the hope they needed.

However, we can't finish our study without looking at one additional thread running through each of these people's lives. **Each one had a choice. Every person we've studied had the option of following Jesus or walking away.**

Mary could have chosen not to have the baby.

Joseph could have chosen not to obey the angel and marry Mary.

The shepherds could have said, "That's too far to walk, I'm too tired," and missed the whole event.

The wise men didn't have to follow the star; the disciples could have ignored Jesus' call and continued their lives as normal.

The Samaritan woman could have walked away from the conversation.

The demoniac didn't have to throw himself at Jesus' feet.

The people whose lives were touched by Jesus could have followed Simon's path and the path of the Pharisees and been either disinterested or repulsed by Jesus. As we've learned through the course of this study, there were plenty of people who did exactly that!

The thief on the cross could have cursed God and died rather than repent. After all, the other thief did.

Mary Magdalene could have chosen to remain a prostitute, wallow in her sin, and miss the opportunity for her life to change.

The truth is that there are two sides to the coin. Throughout this book, we've clearly learned that each human being is significant to God. The invitation to join God's family is open to everyone. The question is, Will you accept the invitation?

Revelations 3:20 puts it this way: **"Here I am! I stand at the door and knock. If anyone hears my voice and opens the door, I will come in and eat with that person, and they with me."**

Today, as in the New Testament, Christ's invitation is an open invitation—extended to everyone. It isn't just an invitation to get into heaven. Instead, these words give the image that repentance from sin provides an invitation—an open door—to a relationship. If you go back and study the original Greek for the word we translate as "eating," it refers to the Oriental tradition of inviting someone over for the main meal of the day for intimate fellowship with the closest of friends. Literally, the words of this Scripture, are an invitation to repent, accept Jesus as your personal Savior and enter into a close, intimate relationship with him.

As we've read about many times, there were far too many people in the New Testament that said, "No thanks, I do not want to have any part of you, Jesus." They walked away and their lives stayed pretty much the same.

Then there were the people who said, "Yes! Yes! Absolutely Yes! I want EVERYTHING that Jesus has to offer and more!" These were the people who sought him out, desperate for his touch. These were the people whose lives were radically changed. These were the ones who found their significance in their Savior.

I don't know what label you're wearing today.

Smart or stupid.
Success or failure.
Popular or rejected.
Attractive or unattractive.
Full of potential or wasted potential.
Sinner or saint.
Easy fix or unfixable.

Honestly, it doesn't matter. In God's eyes, these labels are completely insignificant. In his eyes, you are his daughter: precious and honored. He has created you with limitless possibilities and endless potential. His greatest desire is to take the raw potential in your life and mold it and shape it into the image of his Son, Jesus Christ.

With his strong, capable hands, the Master Potter wants to take everything in your life—your past, your hurts, your failures, your accomplishments, your strengths, your weaknesses, your triumphs and tragedies, and turn them into something beautiful and useable in his kingdom.

Everything you have gone through has not been for nothing. It was training. It had a purpose.

Everything you have gone through has not been for nothing. It was training. It had a purpose. It has brought you to where you are now—standing on the precipice of the greatest adventure of your life. The adventure begins the moment you put your toes in the water and say, "I want to become the woman of God I was originally created to be. I am ready to fulfill my calling—to develop the character of Jesus in my life and become a reflection of him."

If you are willing to answer his call, accept his invitation, put him first in your life, and allow him to do whatever he wants to make you into the image of his Son, he has an amazing plan for you. He's ready for your adventure to begin today.

The only thing left to decide is: Are you ready to follow him? Is he significant to you?

Epilogue Questions

1. **Every person we've studied had the option of following Jesus or walking away. Have you made your choice?**

2. **This chapter says that "Everything that you have gone through has not been for nothing. It was training. It had a purpose." Have you identified the purpose yet?**

3. **Are you ready to follow God? Is he significant to you?**

Notes

Chapter 1

1. Alfred Edersheim, *Sketches of Jewish Social Life.* (Peabody, MA: Hendrickson Publishers, Inc., 1994), 32–33.

Chapter 2

1. Alfred Edersheim, *The Life and Times of Jesus the Messiah.* (Peabody, MA: Hendrickson Publishers, Inc., 1993), 151–162.

2. Ibid., 155.

3. Ibid., 156.

4. Ibid.

Chapter 4

1. Kenneth L. Barker, and John R. Kohlenberger III, *Zondervan NIV Bible Commentary Vol 2: New Testament.* (Grand Rapids, MI: Zondervan Publishing House, 1994), 303.

2. John McArthur, *Twelve Extraordinary Women.* (Nashville, TN: Thomas Nelson, 2005), 153.

Chapter 6

1. Alfred Edersheim, *The Life and Times of Jesus the Messiah.* (Peabody, MA: Hendrickson Publishers, Inc., 1993), 341.

2. Kenneth L. Barker, and John R Kohlenberger III, *Zondervan NIV Bible Commentary Vol 2: New Testament,* 143.

Chapter 7

1. Rev. Richard Herritt is the author of the deliverance prayer. He is the leader of Herritt Spiritual Warfare Ministries, Inc., www.conquerors-in-christ.org.

Chapter 9

1. John McArthur, *The MacArthur Bible Commentary.* (Nashville, TN: Thomas Nelson, 2005), 1157.

Bibliography

Barnes, Albert. *Barnes Notes on the New Testament*. Grand Rapids, MI: Kregel Publications, 1980.

Hayford, Jack W. *Hayford's Bible Handbook*. Nashville, TN: Thomas Nelson, 1995.

Edersheim, Alfred. *Sketches of Jewish Social Life*. Peabody, MA: Hendrickson Publishers, Inc., 1994.

Edersheim, Alfred. *The Life and Times of Jesus the Messiah*. Peabody, MA: Hendrickson Publishers, Inc., 1993.

MacArthur, John. *One Perfect Life: The Complete Story of Jesus Christ*. Nashville, TN: Thomas Nelson, 2013.

MacArthur, John. *The MacArthur Bible Commentary*. Nashville, TN: Thomas Nelson, 2005.

MacArthur, John. *Twelve Extraordinary Women*. Nashville, TN: Thomas Nelson, 2005.

Barker, Kenneth L. and John R. Kohlenberger III. *Zondervan NIV Bible Commentary Vol 2: New Testament*. Grand Rapids, MI: Zondervan Publishing House, 1994.

$\mathcal{A}$dessa Holden is a graduate of the University of Valley Forge and an ordained minister with the Assemblies of God. She is the founder and editor of A Wellrounded Woman Ministries and the co-founder of For a Single Purpose Ministries.

Adessa became a born-again Christian at the age of five, and was raised by a godly mom who taught her and her brother that there was no greater purpose in life than following Jesus. When asked about herself she'll tell you, "I'm a single gal, a woman's minister, a sister, and a daughter. I love to laugh and spend time with friends. I'll eat anything chocolate. I love music, and I'm a bit of a cleaning freak. It is my absolute honor and privilege to serve Jesus Christ and women through this ministry."

Adessa Holden can be contacted at **adessa@awelIroundedwoman.com** or **adessa@forasinglepurpose.com**, where she welcomes any questions, comments, or requests for speaking engagements.

For more information about A Wellrounded Woman Ministries and For a Single Purpose Ministries, or to see how you can help provide resources to help women grow in their walk with God, contact:

4One Ministries
1109 E. Colliery Avenue
Tower City, PA 17980

Or visit www.awelIroundedwoman.com
or www.forasinglepurpose.com